THE CHANGING

St Clements

and East Oxford

BOOK ONE

Susanne Shatford
and
Trevor Williams

Robert Boyd
PUBLICATIONS

Published by
Robert Boyd Publications
260 Colwell Drive
Witney, Oxfordshire OX8 7LW

First published 1997

Copyright © Susanne Shatford, Trevor Williams and
Robert Boyd Publications

ISBN: 1 899536 15 9

OTHER TITLES IN THE
CHANGING FACES SERIES

Botley and North Hinksey
Cowley
Cowley: Book Two
Cumnor and Appleton with Farmoor and Eaton
Headington: Book One
Headington: Book Two
Jericho
Littlemore and Sandford
Marston: Book One
Marston: Book Two
Summertown and Cutteslowe
St Ebbes and St Thomas: Book One
Wolvercote with Wytham and Godstow
Woodstock

Anyone can publish a book — why not you!

Have you ever wanted to publish a book? It is not as difficult as you might think. The publisher of this book provides a service to individuals and organisations large and small.

Advice can be given on all facets of production: typesetting, layout and design, paper stocks, styles of binding including wired, perfect, sewn, limp and cased binding, the options are almost endless. If you have a project you would like to discuss why not contact:

Robert Boyd
PRINTING & PUBLISHING SERVICES
260 Colwell Drive
Witney, Oxfordshire OX8 7LW

Printed and bound in Great Britain at The Alden Press, Oxford

Contents

Cover illustrations

Front: Jack Buckler, Fishmonger and Poulterer,
       Cowley Road, c. 1928

Back: East Oxford School May Celebration 1912

Acknowledgements

We would like to thank the following for their generous contributions, without which we would not have been able to produce this book (and our apologies to anyone we have inadvertently omitted from the list):

Hazel Anderson
Margaret Anderson (N.Z.)
Cyril Beesley
Royston Beesley
Peter Begley
Jean Burch
Pam Blaby
John Blakeman
Marjorie Bristow
Jean Chilton
Philip Copeman
Margaret Cullen
Ernie Currill
Bob Davidson
Les Deacon
Marjorie Foster
Esme Gibb
Les Grant

John Gray
Eric Harris
Frances Harris
Ernie Hine
Glenys Hudson
Nancy Hunt
Jean and Wally King
Stanley and Doreen King
Alan Knowles
David Ledger
Nest Lewis
Jane Madden
Sheila McGuinness
Stella Melling
Beryl Millar
Peggy Naish
Kath Pateman
Roy Pyniger

Bette Reynolds
Daisy Richardson
Ron Robinson
Mary Rodgers
Anne Savin
John Scott
Jean Sheldon
Greta Smith
Doug Stowell
David Surman
Margaret Taylor
Tracey Taylor
Thelma Telling
Gordon Thompson
Fred Townley
Joyce Tyler
Emily Wakefield
Edna Watkins

Nuela la Virtue, Oxfordshire Photographic Archive
Jeremy's P.C.s — Oxford Stamp Centre
Colin Harris, Librarian, Bodleian Library
Ramon Roper for research into the life of E.A. Greening Lamborn
East Oxford and S.S. Mary and John Schools
Dr N. Tiffaney, Oxford City Charities
Father Bean, Society of St John the Evangelist
Sister Margaret (Archivist), St John's Home
Malcolm Graham, Centre for Oxfordshire Studies
Cowley Local History Society
Frank Blackwell, photography

Thanks are also due to:
Wendy Williams for collating information
Anne Prince for proof reading
Adrian Shatford for maps and drawings

Preface

The two parishes of St Clement's and St Mary and St John are situated at the eastern access to the city of Oxford. The ancient parish of St Clement's was well established in the medieval period, and the sprawling Victorian suburb of East Oxford, which developed in what was then part of the original Cowley Parish, provides a fascinating contrast. Initially St Clement's was the dominant community and the new development of the 1850s was dependent on it for all services, schools, church, shops and tradesmen, but latterly, as East Oxford has expanded, this role has been reversed.

The response to our request for photographs and information has been tremendous, as the extensive list of acknowledgements illustrates. We have, therefore, decided to produce two volumes. In this, the first of the two books, we have traced the early development of the two suburbs and covered some of the institutions, services and personalities of the areas based on the information which we have currently received. You, the reader, will of course be aware of the gaps, many of which we hope to fill in the next volume. However, we are still collecting material and would love to hear from anyone who could help us to complete the picture.

St Clement's Church with bell tower before the square stone tower was added in 1816.

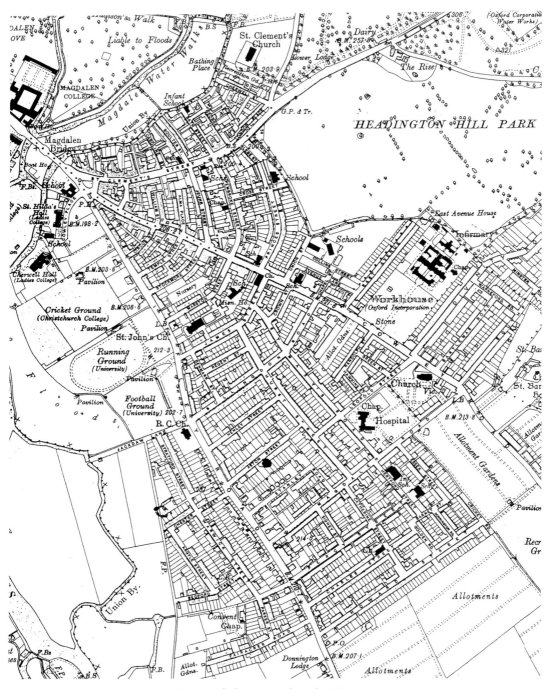

Map of the area dated 1919.

Part One: St Clement's

SECTION ONE

The Plain

The ancient parish of St Clement's dates from Anglo-Saxon times and is referred to in Ethelred's charter 1004 AD. as 'the three hides beyond Cherwell Bridge' (i.e. approximately 360 acres). The medieval manor stretched from the bridge southwards along the Cherwell, eastwards to the top of Headington Hill and south to Cowley roughly following the line of the present Cowley Road. Until the 17th century, the settlement was known as BRUGGESET (Bridge-set), indicating the site of the important river crossing which gave access to the city from the capital. In addition, the settlement which developed along this highway now called St Clement's was known as Bolshipton. The Bolles family had farmed the demesne in the 13th century and their cow bier (shippon) probably occupied the site opposite the Black Horse Inn and provided a local landmark. Bolshipton House occupied the site until 1642 when a substantial number of properties in the area were demolished to make way for the civil war fortifications.

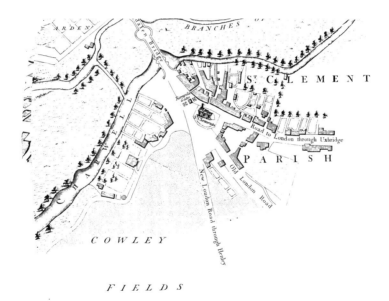

Richard Davis Map 1793—94.

The early settlement expanded rapidly throughout the late Middle Ages as traders and craftsmen settled outside the city boundary thus avoiding the expensive city taxes yet maintaining the benefit of close proximity to the local market. The population further increased in the early 19th century when tenement houses were demolished in Oxford and the homeless sought refuge in the less expensive suburb. The pressure for housing caused a cramped network of narrow streets and courts to develop between the St Clement's High Street and the river. Facilities were non-existent; pumped water was only installed after a severe cholera epidemic in 1832 and mains drainage followed in 1854 after the parish had been annexed to the city in 1835.

The Plain and tollhouse c.1868 with the original Cape of Good Hope on the right. (Bodleian Library, MS. Top. Oxon. d.496, fol 4).

As a result of the Mileways Act 1771, a turnpike was established on the Plain and tolls were levied for use of the road. Prior to this date the responsibility for road maintenance had fallen on the parish, which was a heavy load for poor parishioners and had rendered the highway to London virtually impassable on occasions. The Turnpike Trust removed this responsibility on major routes and continued to maintain the highway until the Trust's abolition in 1868. The tollhouse stood on the site of the present Victoria Fountain in front of the ancient churchyard of St Clement's Church; the left-hand gate controlled the traffic to Headington and the right-hand gate the traffic to Cowley and Iffley.

THE ABOLITION OF THE ST. CLEMENT'S TOLLS.—After an existence of just over a century, the tolls at the St. Clement's Gate were abolished on Saturday night last. The materials of the toll-house were sold the previous day by auction, as stated last week. As midnight approached, a large number of persons assembled at the spot, and immediately the clocks struck 12 loud cheers were given, some vehicles, which had been waiting there for the purpose were driven through, and a few fire-works were discharged. There had been rumours afloat for some days previously that a demonstration would be made when the gates were taken down, but Mr. Hanger, who had purchased them, as a measure of precaution, had them removed from their hinges early in the evening. A few policemen were present, but, after about an hour's amusement among those congregated, the crowd dispersed without their aid being called into requisition. The toll-house is now in course of demolition, and will, be believe, be re-erected by the purchaser, Mr. Fruin, at Toot Baldon, in the same form in which it has existed for so many years.

In 1869, the tollhouse was sold to Mr Fruin of Toot Baldon, who dismantled it and removed it. It is not known whether the house was re-erected or whether the stone was used for other purposes. Excerpt from *Jackson's Oxford Journal* for November 1869.

The installation of the tollhouse was not altogether popular and toll evasion occurred. The owner of the house which stood on the south side of the gate, where Magdalen College School now stands, always avoided paying as he had an entrance to his house on each side of the gate.

Jackson's Oxford Journal records 19th Sept. 1874,

'Mr Jason Saunders of Medley Farm was summoned by Alf Hanger, lessee of St Clement's Toll Gate for unlawfully passing through without paying 2d the toll legally due on the 9th inst. for a carriage with 2 wheels, drawn by one horse. The Mayor said that the said Mr. Saunders had discovered his error and wished to apologise and as Mr Hanger did not press charges, the summons was withdrawn'.

A view of the Plain c.1915 with the new Cape of Good Hope public house on the right in the background and the Victoria Fountain in the centre. Mr and Mrs G.H. Morrell commissioned the design by P.E. Warren in 1899 and it was inaugurated by H.R.H. Princess Louisa on 25th May on the site of the toll house.

On the present roundabout is a stone plaque commemorating the short-lived peace declared on June 22nd 1814 when Napoleon was imprisoned on Elba. It is one of about six stones set up at the time around the city.

The South African War Memorial

The South African War Memorial at Oxford. The Unveiling Ceremony, 19th September 1903.

The South African War Memorial to the memory of the Officers, non-Commissioned Officers and men of the 1st Battalion Oxfordshire Light Infantry, who fell in the South African war, was unveiled by the Bishop of Oxford on 19th September 1903 in the old churchyard of St Clement's (now the Plain roundabout). Four to five thousand people attended the ceremony. As the 1st Battalion were under orders for India in the autumn it was considered advisable to go ahead with the ceremony although the project was incomplete. The monument was designed and executed by Mr Gawthorp, art metal worker, of Long Acre, London, and consisted of blocks of Portland stone, about nine feet high and four feet square with bronze tablets on the sides. (A massive bronze figure of a soldier completed the memorial at a later date.) The front tablet bears an inscription and on the other tablets are the names of those who were killed in action (33) and who died of disease (109).

The Memorial was removed to Cowley Barracks in the 1950s and later to the T.A. Centre, The Slade, Headington.

KILLED IN ACTION

Major: C.R.Day
Second Lieutenants: A.R.Bright
                         V.A.Ball-Acton
Colour-Sergeant: 2568 J.H.Aspey
Lance-Sergeant: 4240 W.F.Meggs
Corporal: 3669 A.G.Walker
Lance-Corporals: 5455 J.Batstone,
                         5686 W.Coleman

Privates
1797 O.Allnutt   5751 T.Appleby
3205 J.Broom   5634 G.Browning
3027 T.A.J.Cripps   3743 A.Davis
3301 J.Goldswain   5445 P.Lawrence
4791 J.Quelch   3934 W.Baker
3719 J.Comber   5822 J.C.Watling
1460 J.Steward   3994 R.Page
3360 C.Floyd   3407 E.Webb
785 C.Woodley   3838 F.Yerby
5878 C.Cripps   5682 P.Delany
5550 G.Pitman   5540 A.Say
3529 G.Crouch   3561 W.Ward
5939 W.Rudge

DIED OF DISEASE

Major: R.W.Porter *Colour-Sergeants:* 2506 G.Olney, 2129 T.Turnbull *Sergeants:* 2478 F.Cadley, 2185 J.Hearn, 2465 C.Clarke, 4195 J.E.Larden, *Lance-Sergeant:* 1966 W.Dudley

Corporals:
3645 J.A.C.Grant   5588 W.Whall   5174 A.J.Constable   5591 A.H.Jones
3982 G.Grove   2903 F.Ward   2155 H.Inder   4246 P.C.Mason
83 W.Boon
Buglers: 4329 R.Lester   5142 H.Wylde
Privates:
6014 E.Avery   4610 G.Archer   3693 W.Baughan   1131 F.Bowles
6005 W.Baldwin   5886 R.Baker   2939 H.Bateman   1494 T.Baker
2781 W.Barton   3036 C.Burgess   5661 A.Boomer   4399 E.Brocks
4931 A.Batchelor   7316 R.Bowles   3380 H.Buck   4452 J.Beckley
3191 A.Brown   2834 W.Brooke   5867 F.Cooper   7320 L.Coulton
3414 F.Cook   2137 F.Coleman   5918 J.Churm   3497 J.Chitty
4098 J.Cloe   5164 G.W.Davis   3782 S.W.Devoisey   3032 F.Eagle
3828 A.Edwards   2455 B.Edwards   3117 J.Faulkner   7303 J.Gould
3586 J.Goodenough   4912 A.George   5525 E.Gardiner   2937 C.Houlton
6546 I.Hamblin   3701 W.Heydon   7233 C.Hobbs   5736 H.Horton
4427 A.Huckins   4433 G.Harris   6533 W.Hutchins   3351 F.Horwood
3631 E.Hunt   3951 A.Huckins   1857 T.Harwood   6107 R.Jones
6284 T.Jones   3278 J.Kentish   2369 G.King   6443 E.Lloyd
3603 W.Lidgeley   4462 A.Maslin   5997 T.Merry   3745 F.Morris
6118 E.Marshall   3423 A.Macefield   6257 G.Nimms   5497 H.Ockleford
2986 J.Portsmouth   5971 F.Puddifoot   5697 F.Penny   3469 W.Quarterman
4629 F.Rickson   2916 F.Rymell   2963 J.Sawbridge   6069 W.Stopp
6263 E.Strong   4284 W.J.Sherman   5903 J.Sparkall   3240 H.Smith
1437 J.Simmonds   5976 A.Staunton   4747 S.Turner   2749 C.Tilbury
5604 G.Townsend   3755 J.Tyson   7331 G.Turton   5357 E.Trinder
4516 L.Vincent   3912 C.Woodbridge 3499 E.Warner   5464 W.Wakefield
5989 G.Wilks   2202 W.Walker   4471 J.Wade   3230 R.Wilson
3136 J.Warner   5532 H.Clarke

The Cape of Good Hope Public House

The original Cape of Good Hope Public House photographed by Henry Taunt in 1892 just before its demolition.

It is believed to have been named after the surrounding meadowland which resembled the outline of the African continent with the site of the Cape projecting out into the Indian Ocean. The Inn probably dates from the 18th century and not only provided accommodation and sustenance for travellers but also offered a weighing service for wagonners wanting to pass through the tollgate. There was a charge of 1d per ton for driving a wagon onto the weigh bridge which was, and still remains today, in the Inn yard. The office can be seen clearly on the left of the building at the entrance to the yard. The Inn was purchased by Mark and James Morrell during the Napoleonic Wars of 1805–1815 and remained a Morrell's Pub until the 1990s.

10	Iffley Road	1		Walter Burgess	Head	M.	27		Licensed Victualar	
	Cape of Good Hope			Edith Do.	Wife	M.	28			
				Mable Do.	Dau.		2			
				Ellen Mole	Serv.	S.	18		General Servant	
				Emily Hinton	Do.	S.	18		Do.	

The family at the Inn listed in the 1891 census.

Walter Burgess was the licensed victualer and can be seen on the steps with his wife Edith and his daughter Mabel. It is possible that the two domestic servants are Ellen Mole and Emily Hinton.

The present building was designed by H.G.W. Drinkwater in 1892 and rebuilt the following year. (O.P.A.)

Fred and Anne Savin were the longest serving landlords this century and kept the pub from 1976 until 1990. They can be seen above at their first Christmas Disco.

Church and School

The original church of St Clement stood at the centre of the medieval village on the Plain. It was founded as a royal chapel at some time before 1122 A.D. when it was given

to St Frideswide's Priory by Henry I. At the dissolution in 1529 it passed to Cardinal College but quickly reverted to the Crown in whose hands it remained until the 19th century. It was demolished in 1830 but the churchyard remained in the middle of the road junction until 1950.

'The parish was poor and populous. In 1800 it contained 400 inhabitants; in 1824 it numbered 2000 and was rapidly increasing. This was partly due to the new canals which, before the railway. brought commerce to Oxford. It was also due to the clearance of closely packed houses from the centre of the city. St Clement's 'sordid by day and by night oil-lighted', stretched from Magdalen Bridge to Harpsichord Row at the bottom of Headington Hill.' (Oxford Apostles by Geoffrey Faber 1933)

John Henry Newman.

In the early 1920s John Newman was appointed curate. He was only 23 years of age but he was given the task of 'recovering the parish' and he set about it with enormous energy. He won the support of his flock who referred to him as 'a proper minister' and a 'nice young man'. The old church, which only seated 200, was now too small to meet the needs of the exploding population, and by 1825 Newman had raised £2,600 for a new building. In 1828 he became vicar of St Mary the Virgin, Oxford just as the new church was completed. He said at his appointment *'It was to me like the feeling of Spring weather after Winter'.* In 1846 he left the Church of England for the Roman Catholic Church, later to become Cardinal.

The present church of St Clement 1953.

The building was erected 1827-28 on land in Nacklingcroft Meadow by Sir Joseph Lock of Bury Knowle House, Headington. It is an exceptionally early example of the neo-Norman style designed by Daniel Robertson and was referred to locally as 'the boiled rabbit'. Most of the £6,500 was raised by public subscription, among the benefactors were John Keble and E. Pusey (friends of John Newman) and the Morrell family.

The three bells from the old church were incorporated; one, dating from the 13th century, is the oldest in Oxford. The present north window is a commemorative glass in memory of James Morrell and was removed from St Martin's Church on Carfax at its demolition in 1896.

A Mothers Union tea party at St Clement's rectory 1920s with Mrs Bird of Boulter Street in the centre front.

St Clement's Church choir 1949.
Back row: Mr Beckett, Mr Shirley, Robert Rolls (curate), Rev Malcolm Kenworthy, –.
Third row: James Burrows (verger), Peter Boyd, Cyril Stone, –, Dickie Bird, Gerald
Shirley, –. Second row: Michael Peacock, Cyril Tennant, –, Trevor Flanakin, –. Front
row: David Hussey, Alan Kirby, –, – Foster, Cyril Teale (organist).

The Girl Covenanters
were a church group
which met in the rectory
on Sunday afternoons
and were organised by
Marjorie Bristow and
Joan Kenworthy. They
are pictured here on their
first birthday in 1948.
Back row: Iris Allday,
Jean Cox, Joy Avins,
Sheila Withy, Vivienne
Lawrence. Third row:
Joyce Howard, Eileen
Brookes, Dorothy Tuck-
well. Second row: Sheila
Giles, Marjorie Bristow,
Joan Kenworthy, Sylvia
Broughton. Front row: Jill
Sturgess, Anne Druce,
Maureen Collett, Greta
Coles, Jean Owens, –.

St Clement's Youth Fellowship c.1950 in the rectory garden. Standing: Basil Hall, Gwen Oxford, Anne Gardiner, Kingsley Mallett, –, Cyril Stone, Wally King, Idris Morrow, Joan Kenworthy, Malcolm Kenworthy (rector), Rupert Hine. Kneeling: –, –, Ron Stone, Sylvia Broughton, Jean Cox, Joyce Howard, Maureen Collett. Seated: –, Josephine Hall, Vivienne Lawrence, Sheila Giles.

A wedding at St Clement's 21st March 1953 between Wally King of East Avenue and Jean Cox of Wingfield ,Street. Back row: Don Sparks, Dorothy Jenkins, William Jenkins, Lily Cox, Ernest Villebois. Front row: Richard Gorrie (curate), Anne Villebois, Pam Allen, Barbara Stone (bridesmaids), Malcolm Kenworthy (rector).

The Church Lads Brigade

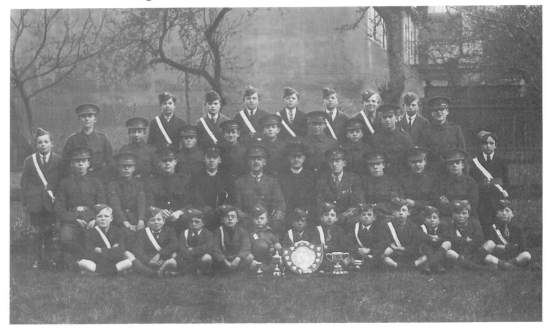

The C.L.B. c.1925 with Ernest Robinson on the far left.

The C.L.B. in 1942 with Stanley King, back row 3rd from left, Peter Green 5th from left and Albert Simmons 1st on the right in the front. Rev. A. Murray Thom and the curate W. Gordon Allison are seated in the centre. The Brigade was essentially a Bible Class which met weekly in the Mission Hall at the top of Boulter Street. They also participated in Church Parades and went on camping trips.

St Clement's Infant School.

There were several schools recorded in the parish in the early 19th century including a Sunday School for 30 in 1818 and a Roman Catholic boarding school in 1830. In 1839 the former Baptist Chapel situated on the western side of George Street, renamed Cave Street in 1928, was purchased by the Church for £525 and converted into a free school. It was funded by £20 per annum from the Dawson Charity.

Derek and Norman Hodges on their grandfather's tricycle, Bath Street, c.1940s.

The Infant School at the bottom of Bath Street on the Banks of the River Cherwell was opened in 1874 on land belonging to the Morrell family. It catered for boys and girls between the ages of three and seven. It opened on the 15th January and the event is recorded below.

> St Clements Infant School. opened Jan 75 1874. J. Knowles. Pupil Teacher St. Thomas National school York.
>
> Jan 5th 45 children were sent from the boys & girls school without even the Register with their names. Admitted 71 besides. So the morning was spent in taking names and addresses. No accommodation for Hats &c caused much delay & confusion. Made a good beginning at lessons this afternoon.

The Head Teacher was Mrs Jane Knowles who remained in post until her retirement at Christmas 1903. She received a silver tea service from the children, teachers and managers, and was succeeded by a Mrs Dawkins.

Annie Wilcox pictured above at her family home, 18 Hurst Street, started as a pupil teacher at the school in 1903 at the age of 13. It is alleged that she was spotted by Mrs Morrell as having a particular talent for teaching and was one of the first intake to train at Gipsy Hill College. She qualified and returned to Oxford. She became Head Teacher at Bath Street and later at St Philip and St James in North Oxford.

Edna Robinson remembers the school in the 1920s.

'I particularly remember the lovely Christmas parties; every child had a gift from the tree and Father Christmas was there. At school across a small bridge, we came into a big field where in the summer the little ones took our camp beds and had a little nap. At 7 years old we went to an all girls school . . . the sexes were never mixed in those days. The girls school was 50 yards from home. We had prizes for being top of the class in each subject. Most of mine were for religious knowledge. I had Bibles and prayer books and Alice in Wonderland twice!!'

The Girls School was on the corner of Bath Street and St Clement's and the Boys School was in Cross Street. The School song below was composed by a teacher.

'United we stand, a merry band of gay school girls are we,
Loyal and courteous, gracious and neat and kind we must always be,
Helping each other, improving ourselves
Playing the game be the role
So now let us sing as the rafters ring
Three cheers for St Clement's School.'

A group of seven year olds in 1916 complete with pot plants. Back row: −, −, −, Denis −, −, −, −, − Barrett. Third row: Kathie Baker, Dorothy Belson, −, − Weller, − Barrett, Marjorie Bristow, John Juggins(?), −, −, −. Second row: Alice Hanger, Lizzie Adams, Alma Timms, Ethel Baldwin, −, Gertie Heritage, −, −. Front row: −, −, − Galloway, −, −, −.

Group 1 c.1934. Back row: 6th from left Bette King. Middle row: 9th Rosemary Selcombe, 12th Vera Payne. Front row: 3rd Dennis Selcombe, 7th Stanley King, extreme right Helen Cullimore.

The whole school taken in June 1952. Staff, from the left: Doreen Goddard (nursery teacher), Phyllis Nutt (helper), –, Marjorie Bristow (head teacher), Myrtle Fry (teacher). Children include: Linda Palfrey, Rita Smith and Maggie Knight.

By 1953 the number of children in the area was dropping and it became evident that the school would have to close at sometime in the future. It was therefore decided to celebrate the 80th anniversary of its opening, which was done with great enthusiasm on 8th April 1953.

The children are pictured above dressed as nursery rhyme characters for the day's festivities.

The staff and the parents at the last Christmas party in 1956 just prior to the closure. Front from left: Mrs Brickwell (cleaner), Miss Marchant (nursery teacher), Marjorie Bristow (head teacher), Miss Baltrip (teacher), Mrs Wells (dinner supervisor).

Marjorie Bristow had been connected with the school for forty years. She started as a five year old in 1916 as she grew up at the lodge of Headington Hill Hall. At the age of eight she transferred to the Girls School and from there won a scholarship to Milham Ford School, then situated in Cowley Place. In 1929 she qualified as a teacher at the Salisbury Diocesan Training College and, after a period in Wiltshire and at the Open Air School in Manor Road Headington, she returned to teach at St Clement's in 1947. The following year she was appointed to the headship and remained until the closure in December 1956. The building was used as a Nursery Students Training Centre.

The Mission Hall pictured on the right was used as the assembly hall for the St Clement's Girls School. The classrooms were above and to the rear and the main entrance was in Boulter Street. Girls transferred here from the Infant School at the age of eight. The school opened in 1891 and closed in 1929.

Alms Houses

Stone's Alms Houses

The Reverend William Stone, principal of New Inn Hall, died in 1685 and left the residue of his estate in his will, dated 12th May, to be used for charitable purposes. From a letter written by Obadiah Walker, Master of University College, who had been entrusted with the execution of the works, we learn that Rev. Stone originally wanted to build a small hospital at Wimborne, Dorset, his birth place. However, he was so worried by the high rate of mortality in the city that he chose to erect the hospital in Oxford. His wishes are made explicit in the said letter to the Provost of Queen's College dated 1st May 1695. '--for sick & poore and none to bee refused as long as there be room to receive them, that it should be founded without reverences upon the providences of our good Lord and the alms of well disposed and devote persons and that all Inhabitants, priveleged or not , strangers, men of all professions, Catholics, Protestants, dissenters should be received and none restricted that were fair objects of such charity.' However, by 1695 arrangements were well under way and 'a hospital with sufficient endowment to maintain three or more impotent persons was a reality. In February 1687 a piece of land was purchased and Bartholomew Peisley, an Oxford free-mason, was appointed to build the hospital for a sum of £250. George Smith, a carpenter from Headington, was also paid £180 for frames and partitions, and the building was opened 20th April 1698.

Bartholomew Peisley's sketch plan of the hospital which was attached to the original agreement dated 27 March 1697. The plan shows ten dormers but according to Hearne only eight were built and none of these remain today.

The first occupants in 1699 were

Gilbert Gardiner	Bookbinder	Judith Bristoe	Widow
Thomas Lawrence	Glover	Hannah Parsons	Widow

The residents were known as the brethren and sisters of Mr Stone's Hospital and were provided with a common seal depicting the benefactor's coat of arms. They were supported by an endowment of land at Gosford purchased in January 1700 and additional bequests in money and kind, e.g. a member of Corpus Christi left provision for a Christmas dinner but this was commuted into additional firing of a ton and a half of coal per annum 1809. At the beginning of the 18th century, Thomas Hearne writes 'the Hospital now supports eight poor and aged women, and is controlled by a Board consisting of six Visitors'. Each widow was provided with £20 per year and an allocation of coal.

Stone's Alms Houses.

This inscription was placed over the entrance to the Hospital at its foundation but in 1823 Philip Bliss recorded 'the old inscription being decayed and rendered illegible, a worthy native and eminent medical practitioner in Oxford Richard Curtis repaired and restored it two years since, having regarded the words 'in hopes of thy assistance' as peculiarly judicious and well chosen'. In addition, he gave money for comfort at Christmas.

The inscription over the entrance to Stone's Court.

Kathleen Griffin, on the right, a resident in the 1980s, said *'I love it here. I don't know what you would want that is nicer than this.'*

Today the alms houses provide sheltered accommodation for 22 residents. The original Stone's building contains six apartments with a guest and community room. In 1960 Parsons Almshouse was erected by University College in exchange for the Almshouses in Kybald Street, which had been founded by John Parsons in 1816. The Mary Duncan Almshouse was built in 1964 by the Trustees of the City of Oxford Charities with money given by an anonymous donor.

The rear of Stone's building in the 1980s with Lilian Hepworth, warden, standing in the garden. Parsons building is on the right. Lilian and her husband Leslie were wardens from 1977 to 1989.

Lilian Hepworth at her retirement in 1989 receiving gifts from Mrs Ollie, a resident of 20 years. In the background are Mrs Foster, Mrs Roberts and Mrs Packer.

The Cutler—Boulter Almshouses

A drawing of the Cutler—Boulter almshouses based on the Buckler print of 1824.

These almshouses were founded under the will of Edmund Boulter in 1736 on two acres of land in St Clement's. They stood on the north side of the High Street facing the highway and covering the site of the present Boulter Street and the adjacent houses to the west. The money for the building and for the support of the six male residents was to be provided from the annual rents of three farms, amounting to £156 per annum. The house in the centre was occupied by an apothecary and his shop, and the large garden was divided into plots, half for the use of the apothecary and the remainder divided between the six occupants. There was a stone plaque commemorating the endowment which said

> 'Cutler Boulter's Almshouses built and endowed by Edmund Boulter junior of Haseley Court in the County of Oxford and Harewood in the County of York esq. To do good to the poor and to wise posterity these almshouses were built and endowed in the year 1736 for a poor, neat, decayed, honest man out of each of the following parishes, Wimple in Cambridge, Harewood in Yorkshire, Wherwell in Hampshire, Hazeley in Oxfordshire, Barling in Lincolnshire, Deptford with Bromley in Kent.'

Edmund Boulter was the youngest grandson of Mrs Boulter, the only sister of Sir John Cutler, Baronet. The almshouses were removed in 1885 when the Charity Commissioners formulated a new scheme for the charity. The portion of the endowment for Oxfordshire is today managed by the City of Oxford Charities.

Shops and Businesses

St Clement's High Street was the main commercial centre in East Oxford before the Cowley Road developed in the latter part of the 19th century and business thrived here until the 1980s when the number of traders decreased.

A view of St Clement's in the 1920s looking east. On the left is Kempson's the Greengrocers. (Jeremy's P.C.)

A view looking west towards Oxford with Boulter Street on the right and the Victoria Cafe on the left hand corner next to the Mission Hall. Stone's Alms Houses are on the left by the tree. c. 1915. (Jeremy's P.C.)

ST. CLEMENT'S ST. (St. Clement's), from Magdalen bridge.

NORTH SIDE.

1 Turrell Walter John M.D. consulting physician
3 Hall Frank, picture framer
4 Abraham Bertram, sports depot
4 Abraham Miss Thora A.L.C.M. teacher of pianoforte
4A, Bough Miss Annie
5 Rembridge Mrs
5 Rembridge & Co. musical instrument dealers, tuners & repairers
6 Austin Miss Jane, registry office
7 & 8 Eagleston & Son Ltd. ironmongers
9 & 10 Milham Ford Secondary School for Girls (Domestic Science Dept)
9 & 10 Haynes Wm. Jn
10 McCabe Miss Joan
11A, Timms Saml
11 Blencowe Geo. H. tailor
12 Blackwell Geo. confctnr
12 Stevens Thos. Michl
13 St. Clement's Post, Telegraph & Telephone Call office (Mrs. Ethel Whitehead, sub-postmistress)
14 Freeborn Walter James & Son, butchers
15 Pamplin C. W. & Son, grocers
16 Grubb R. J. & Co. corn merchants
16 Brown W. H
17 Half Moon P.H. Mrs. L. Ladson
18 Oxford Diocesan Magazine (monthly, 3d.) (A. T. Broome & Son, publshrs)
Uganda Church Review (quarterly 1s.) (A. T. Broome & Son, publshrs)
18 Broome A.T. & Son, printrs

...... *here is York pl* ......

19,20,21 & 22 Hatton Rd. drpr
19A, Smith Hy. Thos
23 Heeley George, hair drssr
24 Butt Mrs. Emily, genl. shp
25 Turner Cornelius Joseph, dining rooms
26 Byard T. & Son, fishmongers &c
27 Clark Edwd. Jn. fruitr
27A, Round Harry G. boat propr
28 Baiden Alfd. Jas. dining rms
29 Sykes Geo. H. wireless engnr

30 THE BURTON ALE STORE, Arth. B. Goldsworthy
31 Hicks Ernest E. fruitr
32 Orchard Arth. hair drssr
33 Gibson Geo. butcher
34 Williams Geo. newsagt
35 & 36 Kempson Wm. J. fruitr
35 & 36 Chamberlain Geo
37, 38 & 39 Slaughter W. & Son, grocers
37 & 38 Slaughter Wltr. R
39 Taylor Alfd

... *here are Penson's grdns* ...

40 Ancient Order of Foresters Friendly Society, F. J. Archer, sec
40 Archer Frederick John & Son, printers
40 Archer Miss Olive A.L.C.M. teacher of music
41 Franks Albert J. clothier
42 & 43 Timbs W. F. & Son, butchers
44 & 45 May Edwin, hardware mer
46 & 47 Meredith Fras. N. draper
47 Barnes Mrs. Ruby C
48 Mansell Arthur, beer ret
49 Hudson Alfred, fried fish shop
50 Sadler Aubrey Hy
51 Mattingley Mrs. Hilda L. shopkpr

...... *here is Caroline st* ......

53 Oddy Herbert O. chemist
54 Green Leonard Wilmott, pork butcher
55 Back Ernest Wm. clothier
56 Chapman Mrs
57 Brooks Miss
St. Clement's Mission Rm Victoria Café (Walt. Jas. Hazell, propr)

...... *here is Boulter st* ......

57B & 58A, Venables & Son, house furnishers
58 Souch Sidney Jn. confr
59 Figg Miss Henrietta, dressma
61 Woodward William George, grocer
61 Spearing Mrs. H. L
62 Honey Wm. beer retlr
63 Sims Albt. Wm
64 Hodges Mrs. Kate, shopkeeper
65 Allen Arthur James
66 Oxford Dairy Co. Ltd

.... *here is Bath st* ....

67 Barrett Jsph. Geo. grngro
68 Hague Mrs. Nellie F. ironmngr
69 Hunt George, baker
70 Waldram William Frederick, boot makr
71 Gough Jesse, tobacconist

73 Palmer Hy. Jas. & Son, who. newsagts
74 & 75 Bayliss T. C. & Co. cycle mkrs
76 The Duke of Edinburgh P.H. Frank A. Lamb
...... *here is George st* ......
...... *here is London pl* ... ..

SOUTH SIDE.

.... *here is Glebe st* ....
Fenn Hy. F. (Havering ho)
Cummings Norman (Glebe ho)
Bailey Mark W. (Ferndale)
Marlow Aubrey F. G. (Churston ho)
Kempson Mrs. (The Boundary)

SUNSET COTTAGE :

1 Lewis Miss
2 Walker Miss
3 Francombe Mrs
4 Brogden Mrs

77 Gough Jesse
78 Wellstood Ernest Frdk
79 Steele Arthur Frank
..... *here is Pembroke st* ......
80 Bradyll-Johnson Rev. Leslie M.A., D.D. Oxon. [rector of St. Clement's, & surrogate] (St. Clement's rectory)
St. Aloysius Roman Catholic School (girls & infants)
82 Port Mahon P.H. Chas. W. Molyneux
..... *here is Jeune st* ....
83 & 84 Godfrey Saml. Jn
Morley Mrs. (The Cottage)
Stone's (Dr.) Almshouses

...... *passage to Alma pl. & William st* ......
86 Leech Henry, tailor
87 & 88 Oxford Co-operative & Industrial Society Limited
88 Beasley Mrs
89 Valters & Co. newsagnts
90 Pimm Joseph
91 Bayliss William
92 Fletcher George Alfred
93 Francis Robert F. corn merchant
93 Francis W. R. A.L.A.A. accountant & auditor
94 Papel Mrs
94 Bailey & Howard, upholsterers
95 West William Oliver
95 West Miss Agnes, pianoforte teacher
96 Harris Mrs
96 Harris Fredk. Jas. tailor
97 Bailey & Howard, upholsterers
98 Oxford City of Technical School (Arth. H. Flemming B.sc., A.R.C.Sc. principal & head master)
99 Harwood Thos. Edwd
100 Viner Geo. Ernest
101 Rippington William
...... *here is Dawson st* ......
102 The Black Horse inn, Wltr. L. Cox
102A Lapworth Cecil B
103 Barden Alfd. J
103 & 104 Hatton Richard, carpet warehouse
106 Bryan Hy. Cecil F. harness mkr
107 Symes Harry, confctnr
108 Haynes Hubert, greengrocer
109 Durham Philip, fishmgr
...... *here is The Plain* ......

The Kelly's Directory entry for 1931. (By courtesy of Reed Information Systems.)

The Black Horse Inn, St Clement's High Street.

The Inn in 1909 with Richard Hatton's Carpet Warehouse at Nos. 103–104 in the background. (O.P.A.)

The stone and slate building dates from the 17th century and until 1836 it was the centre for manorial and parish business. Church wardens and overseers of the poor would manage parish funds and provide such items as workman's tools, clothing for pauper children and apprenticeship fees - local documents were housed here. The stocks stood in the front.

St Clement's Fair in September 1936 outside the Black Horse with Mrs Jessie Howard (centre) and her daughter Joyce (on the horse) from Princes Street. It is believed that the fair belonged to Hebborn's.

Originally it had been a Michaelmas hiring fair but it had never been a large event, *'a very mean thing, of no other account but for children's baubles'* said Hearne in 1723. It had been forced off the road earlier in the century due to increased traffic and ceased altogether in the 1930s.

Richard Hatton, Draper, Nos. 19—22 St Clement's High Street

This picture was taken at the time of the fair, which was a memorable annual event for the local people. It was held during the third week in September in the aftermath of St Giles fair and the school log book 1874—1908 records the early closure on this day as attendance was expected to be so low as to make classes not viable.

> Sept. 22nd 1904.   *The school was closed on Thursday afternoon in consequence of St Clement's Fair.*

Hatton's was established by the 1880s and played an important role in the life of the community. The parish charity, called the Dawson Trust, provided money tokens for good school attendance. They were awarded annually and had to be redeemed at Hatton's in exchange for children's food and clothing, thus supporting their education and physical needs. The children also received a silver medal.

School Logbook 23rd Dec. 1904.
Distributed the Dawson Prize Tickets for regular attendance. Children from St Clement's Parish who made more 300 or more attendances since Sept. 30th 1904, received a ticket.
60 received 5/- tickets for boots & clothing.
37 received 4/- tickets.
14 received 3/- tickets.

About 1921, Richard Hatton opened a carpet warehouse at Nos. 103—104 St Clement's and the drapery business moved to these premises in 1937 when Nos. 19—22 disappeared.

St Clement's shops on the northern side of the road in 1961.

Nos. 41—47 showing Edward Mullis gents outfitters, Timbs the butchers and May's Hardware Shop. Edward Mullis was in business in St Clement's from 1940 until 1976. (O.P.A.)

May's Hardware Shop, 44-45 St Clement's

Edwin May married Emmeline Williams in 1908. Edwin went away to serve in World War I and it is alleged that Emmy saved the army pay that was sent home to her and

stored it safely in the family Bible. When Edwin returned c.1916 the money was used to buy No 44, their first shop. It was stocked with crockery which came by train from the Potteries and was transported by carrier's cart from the station. From there the business expanded.

Edwin May and Emmy with their three sons in 1916/17. Bob, the eldest son joined the business and opened the Abingdon branch of May's carpets and another branch in Cheltenham. Ron, the youngest son, also joined the family business and moved it from St Clement's to the Cowley Road.

A family wedding in 1920 in the back garden of 44–45 St Clement's. The May family were linked by marriage to the Williams family who owned the newsagents. Back row: Bertha Williams (sister of bride who owned the Wool Shop at No. 46), Laura Stephens (friend), Margaret Williams (sister of bride), Emmeline May (née Williams, sister of the bride). Middle row: Cousin Agnes Deveral, Emmeline Augusta Blanche Williams (bride's mother), Lionel Smith (bridegroom), Eda Williams (bride), Aunt Rose Deveral, Miss Smith (groom's sister). Front row: Edwin May, Bernard Smith (groom's brother), George Williams (groom's brother).

A family portrait taken at Christmas 1932 with Edwin, Bob, Ron, Frank and Emmy.

Robinson's General Stores, 51 St Clement's

Walter Thomas Robinson was born at 46 Princes Street in 1887. He married Lilian Martha Eustace who had been born in Sidney Street but grew up at 88 Howard Street. Walter's first job was as a coal porter in Oxford and he had to collect the horses from Port Meadow at 4 a.m., load them up and deliver coal all over the city. He bought the General Store at 51 St Clement's, at the corner of Caroline Street, in c.1920 with a loan of £100. The family lived there until 1928 when Walter opened his London Road store in Headington.

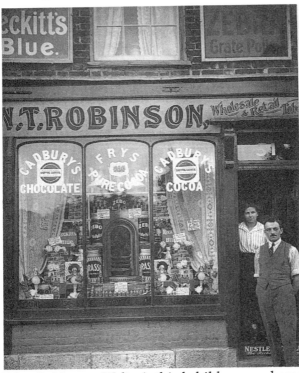

Walter and Lilian Robinson outside the shop c.1912 when they won an award for a shop window display advertising Brasso. Walter delivered coal in the area.

Edna Robinson, Walter's third child, remembers the shop well.

'Most goods for the shop came in wooden boxes which were chopped up and sold as firewood. Lard, margarine, butter and dripping came in wooden boxes. Every ¼lb had to be cut and weighed. Sugar and tea came in sacks and this also had to be weighed. When people came to the shop, they never paid for their goods straightaway; instead it was put in a book and they paid at the end of the week. There was no stock room for the spare goods so most of it was stacked up the stairs with just enough room to get by. We had a cellar under the shop. It had no light so we had to use candles. Dad used to chop wood down there into little bundles and we used to help carry them up to the shop where they sold for 2d a bundle.

At our house in St Clement's, we had just a backyard with one tap and two toilets to share between three families. Our living room was very sparse but above the shop there was a lovely sitting room which was only used on a Sunday and at Christmas. We had a gramophone in it which had to be wound up and sound came out of a big horn'.

The Robinson Family outside their bungalow on the Marston Road c.1926. Walter and Lilian and their five children. From left to right: Ernest, Edna, Betty, Lily, and Doris and Kenny the spaniel. Ronald, their youngest child was born the following year.

Edna remembers

'In the summer on a Sunday, my mother would pack up a day's food and equipment and put it in a wheelbarrow (a large wooden box with two wheels and two handles). My brother Ernie would push it all the way to Marston, where father had a piece of land with a one-bedroomed bungalow which he had built. It had a kitchen range in it and mother would cook us Sunday lunch while the children had a lovely time playing in the fields. Although Dad only had one leg, he played with us a lot. We raced with him and he could even beat us on his crutches. In the afternoon we all had to walk back to the Sunday School. On our piece of land in Marston, dad grew vegetables and plenty of flowers which he sold in the shop.'

E. Hudson, Fish and Chip Shop, 49 St Clement's

Edwin Hudson outside his shop c1912.

Edwin Hudson was born in Bicester in 1867 and moved to 90 Percy Street at the turn of the century. In 1904 he opened the Fish and Chip Shop, which he ran with his wife Rosina for years until her health failed and he decided to move to Rose Cottage in New High Street, Headington (a healthier environment) and opened another shop. Edwin had considerable entrepreneurial talents and was at one time involved in the furrier business; he was also the first person to introduce daylight oil to Oxford and developed a distribution round of 13,000 gallons per year. In later years his shop was converted into a Radio Shop.

Rosina with her three eldest children in the garden at Percy Street in 1901. Clara, the eldest, Edwin, who joined the Australian Army and was killed at the age of 20 in the 1st World War, and Gladys, born in East Oxford in April 1900. They were later to have three more children, William and two who died in infancy in 1905 and 1907.

Edwin's great strength was his devotion to the Salvation Army. He had been converted at the age of 16 or 17 after hearing Clara Fisher preach at the Free Methodist Church in Bicester. He trained at Leicester and became an officer and returned to Oxfordshire. On a wet Sunday night in July 1890, he was arrested with Captain Sprake for preaching in Burford Market Place, and on refusing to pay the fine of one shilling and five shillings costs, he was committed to Oxford jail for seven days where he was given skilly (gruel) and black bread and made to pick oakum. On his release he was greeted by the Salvation Army Band and a crowd of supporters, which caused a traffic diversion.

Edwin aged 99 years in 1966.

Edwin lived to be 99 years old and had a telegram from the Queen Mother but he was better pleased when the Salvation Army Band turned up at his Headington home to play for him. His portrait was painted by Edgar Mills in 1966.

G. Williams, Newsagents, 34 St Clement's

The Williams moved from a property which he rented from Hertford College in 1924 when the lease expired. It stood where the Indian Institute was and is now the History Faculty Library. In Broad Street he had traded in second-hand goods which were surrendered when the students went down. He had originally been a coach builder in Pusey Street. Like many of the St Clement's residents, he was a victim of university

development and from 1925 he managed the Newsagency at No. 34. His daughter Bertha had been crippled with polio at the age of three, so George set her up in business at No. 46 St Clement's in a Wool and Drapery Business. Bertha lived there with her companion Gertie Welford who ran a small Post Office in the Wool Shop.

S. Timbs, Butcher, St Clement's High Street, c.1876–1978

Samuel Timbs was born at Wootten, Oxfordshire in 1846. He came to Oxford and settled in St Clement's where he married Elizabeth (Lizzie) Smith, the eldest daughter of Samuel and Silena Smith from Bath Street. The first record of the butcher's shop at 42 High Street, St Clement's appears in the Kelly's Directory 1876 and the Timbs family continued in business until the shop closed a century later.

Samuel Timbs outside his shop in 1890 with his wife Elizabeth and one of his sons. At this time Samuel had five surviving sons and a daughter, Samuel Stephen, William Frederick, Leslie, Harry, Cyril and Maud. All were born in St Clement's between 1872 and 1890. The name of the assistant is unknown.

Samuel Stephen Timbs, the eldest son, is seen here outside 67, St Clement's on the corner of Bath Street. The family had been operating from these premises in addition to no. 42 since c.1889 when Samuel Stephen would have been 17 years old. He is pictured here in 1899 with his wife Alice.

Samuel senior and his wife were both dead by the end of the century and Samuel junior returned to no. 42 to manage the main shop. He can be seen here with his wife Alice, assistants and delivery cart outside the premises in 1900.

The wedding of Leslie Timbs in 1910. Back row: −, −, −, −, −, −, Harry Timbs(?), Cyril Timbs(?). Third row: −, −, −, −, −, Will Willcox, William Frederick Timbs, Lillian Agnes Timbs, −, −, −. Second row: Alice Timbs, Samuel Stephen Timbs, Elizabeth Timbs, Leslie Timbs (groom), Mabel Agnes Gray (bride, daughter of Albert Edward Gray). Front row: −, Maud Timbs(?), −, −,

William Frederick Timbs (centre) pictured at the Christmas stock market in the 1930s. William was a cattle grader and is said to have been able to judge the weight of a beast by laying his hand on it. On his right is Mr Hatt who was a cattle judge and had a business on the Cowley Road. On the left is another grader, name unknown. William Frederick (born 1874) started his butchery business in Bullingdon Road where he met and married Lilian Agnes Burchell.

In 1900 he bought No. 43 St Clement's next door to his elder brother, and Harry Timbs, his younger brother took over the Bullingdon Road premises. In 1910, Samuel Stephen emigrated to New Zealand because of his health and William took over Nos. 42 and 43 where he remained until his death in 1949. It is alleged that William remembered William Morris mending bicycles in the early days at the rear of No. 43.

Lilian Timbs, the wife of William Frederick, continued in the business after her husband died in 1946. She could still be seen behind the cashier's desk perched on a high stool at the age of 89 in the 1970s. When asked about retirement she said *'I have never thought of it. I am too happy working. It keeps me out of mischief and gives me something to do.'*

Denis Jackson managed the shop for 39 years prior to closure.

William Arthur Timbs the last member of the family in business in St Clement's.

The business finally closed in 1978 after 130 years in St Clement's. William Arthur, son of William Frederick went to farm at Great Milton.

"SAM. S. TIMBS"

**BUTCHER CRAFTSMEN & MEAT SPECIALISTS
86 GUYTON STREET WANGANUI**

Original Family Business (Still functioning) established Oxford, Eng. 1760.

The advantages of this traditional trade knowledge is available to you, for your pleasure and economy.

ROYAL OXFORD SAUSAGES (Plain or Tomato) 6D. PER LB.

Samuel Stephen Timbs, it is alleged, emigrated to New Zealand in 1910 because of his health and continued in the butchery business. The sign on the left comes from his business which was established in 1932. It is alleged that the 'Royal Oxford Sausages' were regularly supplied to Queen Victoria. Stephen's three sons, Samuel John, Bob and Reg all joined the family business. Samuel Stephen advised the New Zealand Government during the war years 1939–45 on sending frozen meat to the U.K. He also wrote extensively about the meat industry.

The Victoria Cafe, 57a St Clement's High Street

These premises are recorded in Kelly's Directory 1889 as the Victoria Coffee House. It stood next to the St Clement's Mission Hall on the corner of Boulter Street In 1923, when this picture was taken it was managed by a Mrs Hazell and was taken over by James Hazell in 1936. It appears to have ceased being a cafe by the Second World War and in the 1960s is listed as the Gospel Book Depot. Since 1976 it has been the Christian Book Shop and remains virtually unchanged.

The Victoria Cafe c. 1923 (Jeremy's P.C.)

The Victoria Football Team 1912–1913. It is believed that the team met at the Victoria Cafe. Back row: 2nd left George Higgs. Seated: 2nd left Henry Higgs.

The Oxford Co-operative Society Ltd.

On October 1st 1874, two years after the establishment of the Society in Oxford, premises in James Street were rented and business commenced in East Oxford. In March of the following year the business transferred to No. 87 St Clement's, a freehold property owned by the Society.

The St Clement's Co-op c.1920. The left-hand window is displaying provisions and the right-hand cakes and groceries (a Co-op classification). Trade was so good that in 1937 the Marston Branch opened to relieve the pressure.

Ernie Currill started his career at the Cowley Branch in 1934 and transferred to St Clement's in 1937. He worked under Mr Osier and Mr George Gibbs; his first position was that of order assistant and it was his responsibility to collect the orders from Morrell Avenue and district. He is pictured on the right at his home on the day that he started work in January 1937, holding a tin of Heinz Tomato Soup. The branch closed in 1970.

Ernie Currill in January 1937.

The General Store 6 Bath Street

Henry William Hodges was born at 34 St Clement's in 1894 and was to become William Morris's original pattern maker at Cowley. He married Mable Russen of the Temple Bar Public House in Temple Street in 1921.

Back row: Clara Russen, Amy Hodges, Arthur Miles (best man), Olive Hodges, Nellie Russen. Front row: Kate Hodges, Henry Hodges, Mabel Russen, Arthur Russen, Elizabeth Russen.

In 1924 they bought a business at 6 Bath Street from Billy 'Soapy' Hudson with contents and furniture for £85.10s.0d. The building was owned by Symmonds Brewery and previous uses had included a bakery and slaughterhouse. The General Store and Off Licence sold beer by the jug and with children in mind, 'vantas'. Vantas was bottled on the premises. The bottles were washed, filled with water, a flavoured tablet added and gas injected, and the fizzy pop was ready for sale. The couple's six children helped in this bottling process.

Mr H. W. Hodges
Bought of Mr H. Hudson

Business and contents of Shop £ s d
6 Bath St. St. Clements Oxford 77 .. 17 .. 7

Furniture in House 7 .. 12 .. 5
£ 85 .. 10 .. 0

Received with Thanks.

10 ... *24*

Henry continued to work at Morris Motors and helped in the shop in the evening until his untimely death in 1936. Mable continued at the shop until 1951 although the licence for the sale of alcohol was revoked on her husband's death. All the provisions for the shop were ordered through salesmen. Mr Johnson used to call once a month with a sample case full of trays of sweets from which Mrs Hodges would make an order. The other provisions come from Twinnings Brothers, Grimbley Hughes, Bales (tobacco products) and Symmonds Brewery for the off-licence sales.

The Hodges children c.1936: Doris (10) Richard (8) Margaret (12) Norman (4) Derek (8) Jean (6). All the children attended East Oxford School although Doris and Derek spent some time at the Open Air School, Headington.

R.T. Harris & Son Ltd (Electrical Contractors)

The founder, Robert Thomas Harris, worked as a colliery electrician in South Wales before coming to Oxford. He worked for the local Electricity Board and then in a partnership before deciding to go into business on his own.

R.T. Harris outside 16 St Clement's.

In 1947 he and his wife, Jessie, took the lease of a lock up shop in St Clement's with a workforce of two electricians and one apprentice. They operated a typical electrical contractors business from the shop, and also sold heating, cooking and various electrical appliances. Their son, Bob, took over the business in the late 1960s.

16 St Clement's.

Expansion took place in 1973 with premises in East Avenue. The two shops were consolidated in the Cowley Road in 1978, in the former premises of Leonard Hughes Ltd. The company left the area in 1990 and moved to Shotover Kilns with a workforce of 74.

The East Avenue shop.

William Matthew Gray, Builder and Funeral Director

William Matthew Gray was born in St Clements parish in 1859 and attended the original Cowley St John School in Iffley Road, run by the Reverend Benson. Gray became a chorister at the Iron Church in Stockmore Street, the income from which helped to pay his school fees. He left school at the age of 14 and worked for his father in the carpentry and joinery business. He later became clerk of works to the Old Oxford School Board and then on his own built up the builders and funeral directors business at 6 Pembroke Street (now Rectory Road).

William as Sherriff c. 1910.

From a young age William Gray had been interested in municipal politics and in 1903 stood for the City Council as a progressive candidate. He was elected with 1231 votes - a record at the time and the East Ward electors never regretted their choice. William took his municipal duties seriously and served on all the hardest worked committees such as the housing, town planning, property and estates, finance and farm committees.

In politics he was a staunch supporter of liberalism and was active in the East Oxford Liberal Club. Other involvements included 40 years as President of the East Ward Allotments Association and the Oxford Movement for helping the distressed Welsh miners.

He was held in great veneration, his home being the meeting place of those in difficulty, particularly those who, following the First World War, were unable to obtain living accommodation.

William was elected Sheriff in 1910 and was finally elected Mayor in 1927.

William as Mayor c. 1927.

William Matthew Gray married twice and had a large family. There were sixteen children. He married Elizabeth Ann Steventon in 1881 and they had twelve children. Elizabeth passed away in 1906 aged 45.

Fanny Katherine Axtell was his second wife. They married in 1907 and had four children. Three of his sons were wounded in the Somme battles and one son, Arthur, was killed.

The Gray family c. 1918. Back row: Tom, Harry, Victor, William, Mathew, Dick, Frank. Middle row: Eva, Bessie, Fanny (mother), William (father), Alice, Dorothy. Front row: Robert, Jean, John, Harold. Inset: Arthur.

On his death in 1931 large crowds gathered on the funeral route from St Clement's Church to Rose Hill Cemetery to pay their last respects to 'Old Bill' as he was affectionately known, one of the best known and best loved of Oxford men.

Some of the tributes paid to him were: *'He was one of the straightest men who ever walked the streets of Oxford and was a man with one of the greatest hearts'* (Dr W. Stobie). *'There is no man who has done more for the benefit of Oxford than Alderman Gray'* (Councillor Pipkin). *'There was no man better loved than Alderman Gray in that 'Little Borough' of East Oxford, as he himself called it. He endeared himself to everyone. He had no party and had friends in every street'* (Mr Butler).

William Gray's success as a business man was reflected in his will as his estate totalled £25,905.17s.7d.

Knowles and Son Builders

Knowles and Son started life in Holywell Street in 1797 when Thomas Knowles from Headington took over a building firm already on the site and it is now believed to be the oldest building firm in the country which has stayed in the same family.

With the Holywell site required for an extension to Wadham College, Knowles and Son moved its headquarters to Pembroke Street (now Rectory Road) in 1952. The site had previously been used as a store for the firm since 1902.

Alan Knowles, then the 16 year-old son of Chairman Guy Knowles, opened the new offices and workshops, and more than 150 employees celebrated the occasion. The firm continued at Pembroke Street until 1966, when further expansion forced a move to its present site in Osney Mead.

Knowles and Son celebrated their bicentenary in 1997 under the leadership of Alan Knowles.

The workforce c.1951. The Knowles family, in the centre of the second row, are Brian Knowles, Mrs Knowles, Guy Knowles, Alan Knowles.

Four of the employees present in 1951 had 200 hundred years' service between them. Fred Axtell, a foreman mason, 65 years; Tom Brownsill, carter, 59 years; Tom Marshall, lorry driver, 53 years; and Sammy Smith, labourer, 48 years.

The Knowles Generations

Thomas Knowles of Banbury
died 1777

Thomas Knowles the Elder
1754–1826

Thomas Knowles the Younger
1781–1856

Edward Nicholls Knowles
1814–1887

Thomas Richard Knowles
1841–1892

Thomas East Knowles
1871–1943

Guy Nelson Knowles MBE
1907–1987

Alan Alden Knowles
1935–

Thomas Edward Knowles
1974–

Long-serving employees celebrate the opening of the Pembroke Street Headquarters c.1951. Left to right: Ted Philips, Tom Brownsill, Fred Axtell and Tom Marshall.

J. H. Grant Ltd.

John Healey Grant was born in Coventry in 1862. On leaving school at 11 years of age, he spent two years as a pit boy. In 1875 he came to Oxford to work for his uncle, John Durham, who was a blacksmith with a forge in High Street. There he learnt his trade working in the open, over fires, in the middle of the road fitting iron tyres to horse-drawn vehicles.

In 1882, at the age of 20, and with a capital of £5.00, he started on his own at 12 Princes Street as a wheelwright and blacksmith. A year later, in 1883, he married Charlotte Faulkner of Beckley on Christmas Day at St Mary and St John Church.

He opened an ironmongers shop in Cowley Road but by 1888 he was declared bankrupt.

The workforce in the Princes Street in yard 1903. Back row: J. Ivings, W. Read, H. Bushnell, – Cleverly, F. Sanders, J. Bedding, F. Grant. Middle row: C. Simpson, 'Corny', G. Gray, J. Bowles, – Palmer, E. Smith. Front row: – Harris, H. Grant, W. Grant, J.H. Grant, – Slater, H. Beck. Seated: H. Grant.

It was nine years before he was discharged of his bankruptcy but he was able to keep the smithy going, making and mending carts, repairing agricultural machinery and doing general blacksmith work, and moved to 64 Princes Street. During the First World War, the Company made steel straps for shell cases, but it was in the 1920s that business really boomed.

With the expansion of the motor industry at Cowley the company supplied parts for the Morris cars. Luggage grids, spare wheel carriers, and wing stays were some of the parts made for the Bullnose Morris, Morris Cowley and Morris Oxford cars.

J.H. Grant also became a steel stockist which was the main activity at a yard in St Mary's Road, purchased in 1926 when the company needed to expand. The company remained a family concern until 1988 when Barrett & Co. took over, the family name being retained by the new owners.

St Mary's Road Yard c.1920. Left to right: B. Currell, W. Hine, A. Ratcliffe and H. Bowerman.

The workforce in Princes Street Yard, 1928.

Alongside the motor industry work, the company began supplying roof trusses, stancheons, steel panels and girders to many local construction firms, including work on early buildings at the car plants.

Twenty-five years Long Service Awards, 1953. Back row: Frank Jeffs Frank Cox (45). Middle row: Sid Harris (47) Bill Alldridge (52) Les Grant (49) Cyril Hill (53) William Biggs (43) Ted Forster (55). Front row: Ernest Price (53) Frank Dennis (52) Fred Gardner (51) Harold Bowerman (46) (the figures in brackets denote total years of service)

Entrance to Princes Street yard.

General ironwork, like gates, railings, and staircases, were always a major part of the company business and the skilled labour force restored many Oxford landmarks such as the gates to Christ Church Meadows.

Staff outing to Bournemouth c.1920s

Staff outing to Cheltenham Races c.1932

Oxford Boys' Club

(Oxford and Worcester College Boys' Club)

Oxford Boys' Club was started at Mrs Mansell's, 52 St Clement's in the early 1930s. The first leader was Basil Jackson who was helped by his brother-in-law, Mr Betteridge. The Club expanded and moved to a room behind Charles Dance's confectionary shop at 7 Cowley Road.

Football, cricket, boxing and other indoor games were the accepted activities for boys' clubs, but the Oxford Boys' Club boasted a harmonica band. The band gave concerts locally and among their performances was one week at the Palace Cinema, Cowley Road as interval entertainment.

Oxford Boys' Club Harmonica Band c.1934. Left to right: Reg Brown (leader), Dave Cox, Bert Stanniford, Reg Harris, Doug Stowell, Norman —, Ron Strange, Ron Bushnell, Ron Penny, Harry Godfrey, Dick Cullimore, Alec Goodwin.

Mr Thurley took over the running of the Club and during the mid-1930s the Club was invited to a week's holiday as guests of The Miners' Welfare Holiday Camp at St Athan, South Wales, where sporting activities were on the agenda. The Club moved yet again to a room in Milham Ford School in Cowley Place.

On holiday in South Wales c.1935.

The Club Football Team, South Wales c.1935. Back row: Jimmy Brown, — Collier, Len Phillips, Doug Stowell, Rol Badcock, Ron Shepherd. Front row: Ray Mansell, Dixie Green, Reg Brown, Ron Strange, — Fitzgerald.

It was not until the early 1940s that the Club found a permanent home at 98 St Clement's and became affiliated to the N.A.B.C. Students from Worcester College helped with activities at the Club and the name of the Club was changed to Oxford and Worcester College Boys' Club. Len Laishley became leader at the Club, a position he was to hold for many years. The Club thrived during the 1950s and 1960s in a buoyant Boys' Club scene in Oxford.

Under 16 Team c.1957. Back row: Jock Davidson (Manager), Mick Walton, Mick Foreman, Tony Buck, Eddie Aries, J. Norris, D. Merritt, Nigel Brett. Front row: J. Gardner, Doug Foreman, M. Madden, Robert Davidson, Ian White.

Oxford Sunday League Side c.1968–69, winners of the Sunday League Div. 5 and the Jack Sadler Cup. Back row: B. Cole (Manager), D. Quainton, P. Hamp, M. Lee, B. McCormack, D. Pittaway, D. Millward, E. McCormack, R. Green, L. Laishley (Club Leader). Front row: J. Alcon, D. Northover, G. Hamilton, P. Walton, G. Brammall, P. Begley, J. Clack.

Personalities

Edwin Mawer, Bath Street Off-Licence

Edwin Mawer lived at No. 10 Bath Street, opposite New Street. He worked at the Bodleian Library during the day and, with the help of his wife Florence, managed the Morrell's Off-Licence in the evenings. His grand-daughter Marjorie (Midge) recalls seeing customers about 1916 coming to the shop with jugs to collect the beer. The women would hide their jugs under their aprons as it was not considered seemly for them to drink alcohol. Edwin is pictured on the left in 1915, dressed smartly for work, with his wife Florence and his grandson Sidney Mawer. Sidney was the son of John Edwin Mawer and Elizabeth Fanny Hopcroft. John was reported missing, believed dead, in 1915 and the army stopped sending his pay. This left the family in financial difficulties so that Sidney, being the eldest, went to live with his grandparents in Bath Street. It turned out that John had survived the attack and had been transferred to an army hospital. Unfortunately the hospital was blown up and he never returned. Edwin also lost another son, Ernest, in the war.

Elizabeth Mawer with her three children, Sidney, Marjorie and Roy in 1914.

John Edwin Mawer with his brother Arthur at the time of John's marriage to Elizabeth Hopcroft in 1906. Arthur was the only son to survive the First World War.

Edwin, Florence and Sidney Mawer in 1915.

James Richardson, Postman, 61 Princes Street

James Richardson was born in 1882 and is pictured here in Princes Street c.1918 with his son Ronald.

Catherine Richardson, dressmaker, with her two daughters, Doris and Daisy in the garden of their home.

Daisy and Doris c.1911. Daisy became a tailoress and worked for Adamson's and Shepherd and Woodward. Doris became a cashier in St Giles.

61 Princes Street was built in 1858 on land purchased from Pembroke College.

Part Two: East Oxford

Introduction

The Victorian suburb of East Oxford developed as a medley of small streets leading from the 'back-bone' of the Cowley Road during the second half of the 19th century. In 1849, with backing from the Liberal Party, the National Freehold Land Society was formed. The Society's main purpose was to wrest political power from the dominant landowners and this they achieved by purchasing land, dividing it into plots valued at 40 shillings and selling these plots off to people who had hitherto been tenants. Thus '40 shilling freeholders' were established and political support gained by the new freeholders' entitlement to vote. The Conservative Party followed suit in 1852 with their Conservative Land Society which enabled of the working man to own property.

Cowley Road vista from the Plain c.1900 (Jeremy's P.C.).

In November 1853 the National Land Society made their first purchase of land which was to become Alma Place (named after the victory at Alma in the Crimea in 1854). The site was divided into plots 11 feet wide and sold off either individually or in multiples of two or three. Thomas King, an Oxford College servant, bought plots numbered 17–19 and built 7 Alma Place. The individuality of the purchasers remains evident in the variety of housing in each street. Therefore a new era in home ownership was established and this facility was increased in 1860 by the establishment of the Oxford Working Men's Building Society *'to enable thrifty working men to purchase freehold plots for gardens or building'*. Membership was achieved by the payment of a small entrance fee and ownership was reached after six years at one shilling a week.

The schemes rapidly developed as follows.

1853   Marston Street was laid out.

1857–64 Private developers realised the potential investment.
        William Gunstone, a college servant, laid out William Street.
        Sidney Smith, a Cowley yeoman, auctioned off plots that were to become
        Catherine Street, Percy Street and Charles Street. Many were obtained by
        building societies, others being sold on to William Henry Howard,
        auctioneer and estate agent.

1858   15 acres were purchased from Pembroke College for £4,468 and plots were
        auctioned to create Pembroke Street (now Rectory Road), Cross Street and
        Princes Street.

1859   Fairacres Estate and the Magdalen Road were laid out.

Cowley Road, near Marston Street c. 1900 (Jeremy's P.C.).

1864   Land owned by the Hurst family became James Street and Magdalen Road.
        Plots in Hurst Street, Bullingdon Road and St Mary's Road now worth £120.

1868–77 Rev. Richard Benson purchased land for parish use.

1889   Walter Gray bought land from Donnington Hospital for £2,817 and built
        Essex Street and Hertford Street.

Cowley Road, near James Street c.1900 (Jeremy's P.C.).

East Oxford c.1920.

St Mary and St John Church

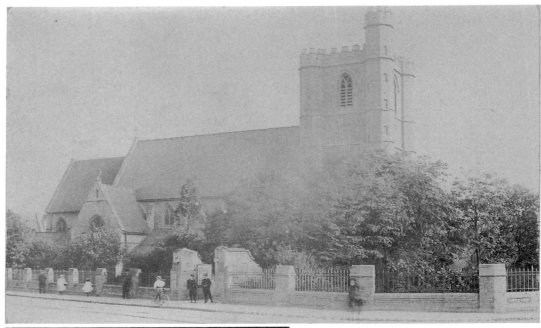

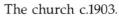
The church c.1903.

St Mary and St John Church was built on land acquired by the Reverend R.M. Benson, Vicar of the Parish from 1870 to 1886, and was based on traditions of the Oxford Movement. The Church was designed by A. Mardon Mowbray and was built of Charlbury stone in early decorated style, the foundation stone being laid in 1875. Construction of the church took many years due to the lack of finance. The original plans included a spire but this and much of the design for the interior was never completed.

The floodlit tower celebrating the Silver Jubilee in 1935.

Celtic Cross commemorating Members
of the Society of St John the Evangelist.

This cross was erected in the grounds
in 1917, commemorating the Reverend
Richard Meux Benson.

1879   The chancel was com-
pleted and dedicated to
Archbishop Longley of
Canterbury, a former
Vicar of St James, Cow-
ley.

1883   The nave and side ailes
were completed and the
church consecrated.

1893   The tower and south
porch were completed
and the adjacent parish
rooms by Bucknall and
Co. were added.

1901   Vicarage house built to
designs by Comper.

1911–12 Vestries added to the
east end.

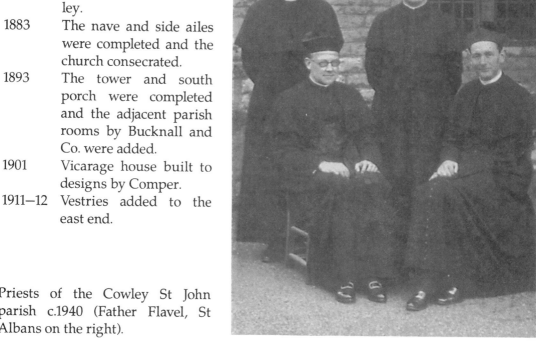

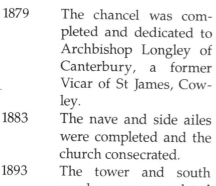

Priests of the Cowley St John
parish c.1940 (Father Flavel, St
Albans on the right).

St Mary and St John Church outdoor service held outside 41 Percy Street c.1915.

The clergy and congregation c.1968.

St Mary and St John Church parish rooms became the centre for many community groups, including Scouts, Guides, Cubs, Brownies, Boys' Brigade, Mothers' Union, and also for fund raising activities, including bingo and jumble sales.

The Boys' Brigade at summer camp, Seaton Devon c.1910.

Members of the Boys' Brigade and cricket team c.1912.

St Alban's Church

St Alban's is part of the parish of St Mary and St John, and in 1886 its first building was a Mission Room on the corner of Catherine Street and Howard Street. The present site on the corner of Charles Street and Catherine Street was purchased by Bishop Talbot of Keble College, Dr Bright, Professor of Ecclesiastical History, and Canon Myers, Principal of St Stephen's House, in 1889 and was dedicated on 30th May. Between 1893 and 1896, the nave was used as a junior school for boys until the completion of St Mary and St John School in Hertford Street.

Margaret Taylor leading the guides past the old Mission Hall next door to the vicarage c.1960. The hall and house were sold in 1984 to a photographer.

The congregation soon outgrew the church and a corrugated iron extension was added in 1911. The vicar at that time, Fr Alfred Cecil Scott, had hoped to raise £5,000 to build a new church but this did not materialise until the 1930s when Lawrence Dale, architect, designed the present church.

St Alban's church interior with congregation in the 1960s.

The entrance is crowned by a pair of angels carved by John Brookes, a local artist who later became the Principal of the Technical College. Under his leadership, the college developed into the Oxford Polytechnic in 1970 and his work was commemorated in the name of Oxford Brookes University in 1992 when the Polytechnics were upgraded.

The church also proudly houses the stations of the cross carved on slate by Eric Gill. The other set by this great artist can be seen in Westminster Abbey. Unfortunately Eric Gill died in 1940 and did not survive to complete the set. The last five stations were finished by his son to Eric Gill's designs and were all finally in place in 1945. It appears that Eric Gill became very fond of this parish and therefore allowed them to purchase the stations at a greatly reduced price of less than £100!

The altar backdrop is usually a tapestry curtain, designed by Grierson in 1949. This hides an earlier mural by Peter Greenham depicting St Alban's vision of the Risen Christ. Because both men are depicted almost naked, it was covered so that worshippers would not be distracted.

Frank Ackerman was a loyal parishioner and organist at the church for most of his life. He gave his services freely and on his death in 1990 he left his house in Fairacres Road and his estate to the church and this has enabled the building to be re-roofed, the Chapel of the Upper Rooms to be refurbished and the organ overhauled. He attended mass at the church every day of his life and died just before his 90th birthday. The parishioners remember him with great affection and gratitude.

Frank Ackerman, aged 6, in 1907.

The Church Choir in the late 1960s. From the left: ?, Nest Lewis, Ian Mitchell (back), ?, Stephen Wyatt, Kim Blackstock, Paul Mitchell (back), Bonitta Blackstock, Susan Wakeling, Jane Bradshaw, Karen Blackstock, Frank Ackerman, Helen Bradshaw, Lucy Jeffery.

The 6th East Oxford Guide Troop, based at St Alban's Church.

6th East Oxford c.1949. Back row: Margaret Taylor, Mavis Blakeman, Enid Bradbury, Jean Parkham, Georgina Proudfoot Jean Blakeman, Joy Walker, Lesley Smith(?), Edna Wiblin. Third row: Janet Smith(?), —, Pat Honey, Daisy Randall (Capt.), Dorothy Brown (Ltn), Mildred Stanley, Maureen Bloxham, June —. Second row: Sally Brown(?), Marilyn Whitley, Mavis — , Jean Randall, —, — Mason. Front row: Janet Young, Anne Smith(?), — Bayliss, — Mason, — Bayliss, — Gray.

The Guides and Brownies standing as guard of honour at the wedding of Mavis Blakeman, the Brownie Leader who lived at 21 Percy Street. She married Ian Bower on 16th November 1957. The officers in the foreground are Anne Reynolds with the Brownies and Margaret Taylor (Guide Captain) with Guiders Susan Long and Carol Roberts and Brownie Sheila Bampton.

The St Alban's Brownie Pack which raised money for Helen House in July 1983. The adults from the left are: June Franklin, Mother Frances Dominica, Jenny Price. The Brownies include: Wendy Allsworth, Alice —, Helen Miller, —, —, Paula —, Karen Elms, Anne-Marie Collins, Joanne Leggett, —, Wendy Smith, Elizabeth Price, Linda Elms, Rachel Price, Nadine —, Kirsty —, Camilla —, —, —, Lorraine —.

✿ HELEN HOUSE
a hospice for children

Helen House
37 Leopold Street
Oxford OX4 1QT
Tel: Oxford (0865) 728251

1st August, 1983.

Dear Brownies,

Thank you very much indeed for the generous gift of £27.20 for Helen House which you raised for us by holding a five mile sponsored walk to Wolvercote. It is so kind of you all to help us in this way and we are very grateful to you, and of course, to all your sponsors.

We are getting to know more and more children and their families and most of them seem to look forward to their visits to Helen House. Tish, our puppy, is a great favourite and she has now been joined by two rabbits. Fortunately they all seem to be good friends!

With our love and many, many thanks,

Mother Frances Dominica

The Cowley Fathers

Richard Meux Benson became Vicar of Cowley in 1851 in a thinly populated parish of about 600. This situation did not last, however, as a few years later there was a rapid expansion of dwellings in East Oxford. To cope with this rising population, Benson had a temporary building of corrugated sheet-iron erected in Stockmore Street which became known as 'The Iron Church'. It was dedicated to St John the Evangelist and opened in 1859. Father Benson left a priest in charge at Cowley and moved closer to his new parishioners.

The Reverend Benson.

In 1866 Father Benson, with assistance from Simeon O'Neill and Charles Grafton, founded the Society of St John the Evangelist (The Cowley Fathers). In 1868 they moved into the Mission House in Marston Street. By 1869 Benson had resigned as curate of Cowley to become the vicar of the fast growing Cowley St John parish. He kept this post until 1886, by which time his parochial work had declined and he the resigned pastoral charge of the district.

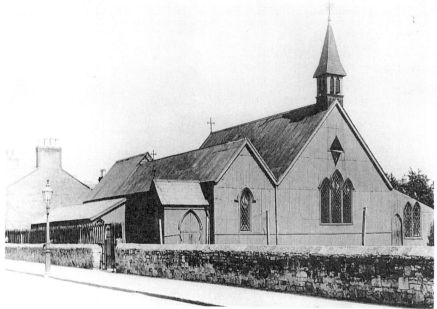

'The Iron Church', the first church of the Parish of Cowley St John. In later years it was the target for local youths who would clatter stones on the roof to disturb worshippers.

By this time, St Mary and St John Church had been dedicated but the Iron Church remained for his use and that of the other fathers. Benson then travelled abroad on various missions for nine years. When he returned, the conventual church of St John the Evangelist had been completed (1896) next to the Mission House. Benson remained there through years of failing health until his death in 1915.

The Mission House, Marston Street.

Father Benson (seated centre) with the Cowley Fathers c.1900.

The rear of the Mission House and St John the Evangelist Church.

St John the Evangelist Church and Cloisters.

The Cowley Fathers vacated the Mission House in 1980. Since then the premises have been occupied by St Stephen's House, an Anglican theological college in the catholic tradition.

The Cowley Fathers leaving their Mission House in Marston Street to attend the dedication of St John the Evangelist Church 1896.

St John's Home

(1873–91, Charles Buckeridge and J.L. Pearson)

St John's Home was founded in St Mary's Road in 1873 for people with lingering sickness or other incurable disease. The land was given by the Reverend R.M. Benson, the Founder and First Superior of the Society of St John the Evangelist. The foundation stone was laid on May 6th 1873 by H.R.H. Prince Leopold, then an undergraduate at Christ Church. Miss Frances Sandford acted as First Matron until 1881.

St John's Home c. 1932.

In 1881 the community of All Saints Sisters of the Poor was invited to take charge of the hospital. This they did, and in 1893 the Sisters became entirely responsible for the work. The first building was designed to take eight patients but, later, extensions were provided. Now the Sisters occupy one half of the large house and run the other half as a home for approximately 40 elderly residents. A chapel, designed by Sir Ninian Comper, was dedicated to St John the Divine and All Saints on 2nd October 1907.

St John's Home
Frontage c.1900.

Sisters   and
patients c.1900.

Sisters at Service
in   the   Chapel
c.1970.

The Garden
Hermitage
c.1900.

The Chair of St Peter in the Gardens
c.1900.

Thomas Wakefield (with wife Emma) the
first gardener at St John's Home. He gave
33 years service and was known as
'Daddy' by the Home.

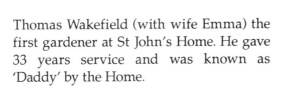

Personalities

Miss Nancy Hunt, Shoemaker, Centenarian

Miss Nancy Hunt was born at 24 Marston Street in 1896. There were 9 children in the family, Nancy being the youngest of six daughters. The family moved to Denmark Street when Nancy was 6 years old. Nancy attended East Oxford School and Sister Alice's School on Sundays.

Nancy aged 100.

The family took it for granted that the young ladies did not learn a trade as their place was in the home. During the First World War, however, Nancy worked at Mintys factory in Cherwell Street, St Clement's making shell carriers. After the war she returned to helping her mother in the home. Nancy always wanted to learn a trade and would watch her father in his shoe-making business. One day, when her father was out, Nancy decided to repair her own shoes. One of her father's customers called, saw the work she had done, and offered her work. Nancy finally got her wish and became a shoemaker in her own right, working in the front room of their house and in a shed in the garden. In 1925 Nancy made three pairs of tiny shoes, one pair of red, one pair of white and one pair of blue, and sent them to the Queen for the Queen's dolls house. At the outbreak of the Second World War Nancy gave up shoe-making to help her mother with refugees from London who lodged at their home, and never started again. Nancy celebrated her 100th birthday as a resident of St John's Home.

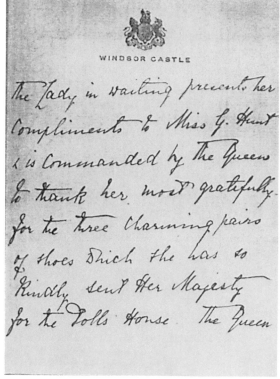

A 'thank you' letter from the Queen's Lady in Waiting.

Henry Taunt (1842–1922)

Henry William Taunt was born in St Ebbes in 1842, son of Henry Taunt, plumber and glazier. Taunt received little schooling, due to frequent truancy, and on leaving school he worked for his father. He did not like the idea of being a plumber and in 1853 joined a tailor's in the High Street; work for a stationer and then the book shop and auction rooms of Charles Richards followed. Taunt enjoyed his work in the auction rooms and stayed for two years.

At Rivera in 1910.

In 1856 Taunt left Richards to join Edward Bracher, who was a pioneer of photography in Oxford. This turned out to be Taunt's vocation and he worked his way up to photographic manager by the time the business changed hands in 1863. Taunt was ambitious and by 1868 had set up his own business. He moved his business around the City as it expanded and Taunt became a famous photographer in the Oxford area.

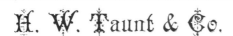

Rivera, 1910.

Handicraft Room
at 'Rivera' 1910.

In 1889 he leased Canterbury House in Cowley Road (more recently part of the Oxford Bus Company) and established a photographic and printing works in the grounds. He re-named the house 'Rivera' after one of his main loves, the River Thames. His distinctive figure was well known to the children of East Oxford, who called him 'Old Skelly Taunt'. Taunt remained at 'Rivera' until his death in 1922.

Taunt was always willing to make his opinions known in public and he was a firm believer in keeping party politics out of local government. His concern about social conditions in the City led him to stand, unsuccessfully, for Council in 1880 and 1881. However, he remained outspoken on local matters as the circulated letter shown on the opposite shows, although his threat to stand for Council again did not materialise.

William Richard Morris, Cycle Maker

The Morris's family home, 16 James Street.

On leaving the church school at Cowley at the age of 14 in 1891, William Morris became apprenticed in the bicycle repair trade. It did not take him long, however, to realise he could make far more money working for himself. Therefore, in 1892, with a capital of £4, he set up business in a shed at the back of his parents' home in James Street. One of the front rooms became his showroom and shop. He started repairing bicycles and selling accessories, then progressed to building his own machines.

Mr F. Pilcher, then Rector of St Clement's, gave him his first order. The Rector was a very big man and required a 27-inch frame. Personal recommendations from Mr Pilcher helped improve Morris's business.

To make the best use of his money, stocks and expenses were kept to the minimum and he even cycled as far as Birmingham to get components. 'William Richard Morris, Cycle Maker' appeared in the Oxford Commercial Directories in 1896–97. By 1901 business had expanded to include 48 High Street and soon afterwards a site in Longwall. The James Street premises were probably still in use until his marriage in 1904.

The Morris Family c.1896. Standing: Alice and William. Seated: Emily, Frederick, and daughter Emily.

The first cycle built by William Morris with a special 27-inch frame.

Not only did William Morris make cycles, he was an avid racer. In his late teens and early twenties he was the cycling champion of Oxfordshire, Buckinghamshire and Berkshire. He won the Oxford City One Mile and the Oxon Fifteen Mile titles in 1899 and 1900 before retiring. The races were not held again until 1903 and in order to retain the trophies outright, he came out of retirement to defend his titles. Extensive training brought success at the Iffley Road running track, Morris taking both titles, but he never raced again. His cycling medals took pride of place over the fireplace in his office for the rest of his life.

Elizabeth Anstey, a school teacher and daughter of an Oxford furrier, married Morris in 1904.

Ivy Smith (née Whitford), centenarian

Ivy Smith was born in Market Street in 1897, the daughter of Frank and Edith Whitford. Weighing only 4½ pounds at birth, Ivy had to be wrapped in cotton wool soaked in olive oil to keep her alive. Ivy's father Frank was a hairdresser by trade.

A Whitford family outing at Boars Hill c.1908 with mother Edith (centre) and Ivy (second right).

When Ivy was four years old the family moved to 27 St Clement's. Business in St Clement's was competitive with five hairdresser's shops and mother Edith took in sewing to help make ends meet. Ivy attended East Oxford School and on leaving worked for Mowbrays and Co. Ltd in the High Street as a seamstress.

Ivy c.1913.

The Whitford family c.1915 at 250 Cowley Road. Standing: Ivy, Frank, Reg, May. Seated: Edith (mother), Gladys, Frank (father).

In 1906 the family moved to 250 Cowley Road, opposite the Workhouse, and in 1918 moved to a shop at 131 Cowley Road. In 1921 Ivy married Frank Smith, Assistant Librarian at Queen's College, at St Mary and St John Church and the couple settled in Stratford Street.

Frank and Ivy's wedding in 1921. Back row: Frank Whitford, Edith Whitford, 'Mother' Smith, Reg Whitford. Front row: Gladys Whitford, Frank Smith, Ivy Smith, Frank Whitford, Ivy Smith (Frank's sister).

Like many families in the East Oxford area, the Smiths took in undergraduates to help supplement the family income. Ivy had two children, Kathleen and Roy, and 50 Stratford Street remained the family home until the early 1960s. Frank died in 1962 and a few years later Ivy moved in with son Roy and then, in 1973, to Jingle Cottage, Marston Street, with daughter Kathleen. Ivy remained there until a few weeks before her 100th birthday which she celebrated in Green Acres Nursing Home, North Oxford.

From the left: Ivy, with daughter Kathleen, Edith Whitford, and Edith's mother (Grandma Gilder) c.1922.

Ivy, 100 years old, in May 1997.

Recreation

The Recreation Ground, Cowley Road

In 1892 a meadow on the Cowley Road (land now bordered by Howard Street, Shelley Road and Cricket Road) was leased by the Council as a recreation ground. The recreation ground was well used by local people, although not always in a sociable manner. In 1897, a high stile was placed at the entrance opposite Henry Taunt's house, 'Rivera'. Taunt complained to the Mayor that the stile prevented old people, ladies and young children from entering the area. Also of concern to Henry Taunt was the use of the stile in the daytime by *'young roughs'* as a meeting place and at night by courting couples for purposes which *'are usually done in dark corners'*. Taunt's letters went unheeded and he further wrote that, on one Sunday near,ly two hundred lads and children had sat on the stile and, on another occasion, *'the night was made hideous by a girl and man at the stile ... I need say nothing about language used, which was both in the evening and at night, of the most debased character, revolting in every way'*.

A shepherd with his flock c.1900 (Henry Taunt's 'Rivera' in the background).

By the Spring of 1898 no action had been taken and Taunt made one last appeal about the stile, threatening to write to the press, *'and if it does not do any good, I shall quietly saw it down'*. The outcome is unknown. Henry Taunt had further complaints about the use of the recreation ground in 1908 (see page 80).

During the late 1920s/early 1930s Mr Lardner, who had a hut on 'the rec', was employed by the Council to keep control. The area continued to be a meeting place for the local youths, with Sunday being the day for six-a-side football.

Cyril Beeesley, 'Ginger' King, 'Nuggy' Burden, Ron Higgs c.1930.

Standing: Horace Whitman, Jack Stanton, 'Bricky' Abbey. Seated: Charlie Beesley, Ted Abbey, Trafford c.1925.

Back row: 'Scroggs' Beesley, Wally Simms, Ron King, Gordon Page, —. Front row: 'Nigger' Caunter, Cecil Higgs, Murcot Higgs, 'Cakey' Brown, 'Nuggy' Burden, — c.1930s.

Greyhound Racing

Greyhound and pigeon racing featured as hobbies for the young men of the East Oxford area. Prize money won was a great help when they found themselves out of work. They used to run their dogs at 'Banger' Hardings track at Cowley.

Bill Beesley with 'Snowy'. Never won a lot — but tried. c.1930.

Sid Abbey with greyhound 'Go-It' and Cyril Beesley with whippet 'Greta' bought for 25 shillings. It won 13 races (prize money 5 shillings) and 1st and 2nd grade Whippet Cup. c.1930.

Oxford Physical Culture Club

The Oxford Health and Strength Club was founded in Oxford in 1925 and was associated with the Health and Strength League. The first headquarters were in a room over the bar of the Grapes Public House in George Street. With the influx of Welsh people to Oxford seeking employment at the Cowley factories in the late 1920s, membership increased. Many of the Welsh sporting enthusiasts were drawn to the club and new activities like weight lifting, boxing and acrobatics were introduced.

Oxford Physical Culture Club c.1937.

Stan Davies, Evan Harris, Billy Cooper, George Brookes, Gilbert Aries, Syd and Gwyn Williams, Evan Morris and Gwyn Morgan were all prominent in the new sections.

Larger premises were required and the Club moved to an enlarged hut on the Cowley Road at the residence of member George Booker. The Club changed its name to Oxford Physical Culture Club.

The gymnastic section gave displays at local fetes and concerts in the area and also entered competitions associated with the Health and Strength League. The Club again outgrew its premises and the headquarters were moved to the Labour Hall, Pembroke Street. St Mary and St John Infants School was also used. The weight lifting remained at Cowley Road while the boxing used Iffley Institute.

A training session at St Mary and St John Infants School, Hertford Street c.1937.

In action at a local fete.

The original 'Alfresco Five'
c.1935–6

Percy Ewers   Horace Gilec
Evan Harris   Danny Behan   Bill Wilkins

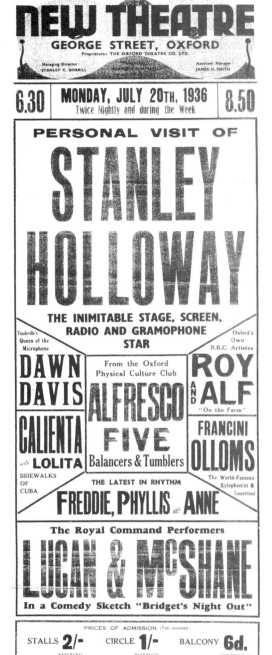

Five of the more accomplished gymnasts formed a group called the 'Alfresco Five' with Vic Couling as Manager. Engagements included the London Palladium, the Holborn Empire and two weeks at the New Theatre, Oxford (now the Apollo).

Esme Harris, Olympian

Esme lived at 111 Morrell Avenue and attended East Oxford and Central Girls' Schools. She was an accomplished gymnast from an early age, due to her father's involvement with the Oxford Physical Culture Club. When Esme had learnt to swim, her gymnastic ability steered her towards diving. At the age of nine, and a member of the City of Oxford Club, she became County Diving Champion, a title she was to win more than twenty times. It was while competing in the National Championships at Hastings in 1947 that her potential was spotted by coach Milly Hudson who encouraged Esme to train once a fortnight in London with Hammersmith Ladies and under whose guidance National standard was reached. In June 1948 Esme, then 14 years old, won the Olympic trials and with the national Championships cancelled, was selected to represent Great Britain at the London Olympics in July. Hopes for a second Olympics in Helsinki in 1952 were dashed, Esme missing a top three selection spot by one point.

Her father, Evan Harris, on a trampoline erected in their garden to help Esme with her training.

Gaining a head for heights at an early age Esme (6) on her father's shoulders supported by Ted Scoones.

St John's Boys' Club

Following the work of the Society of St John the Evangelist with Sunday schools in the parish of Cowley St John, it was felt that more was needed for young people in the area. Father Podmore was the instigator in forming St John's Boys' Club for sports of various kinds in the 1930s in Marston Street.

Boys' Club table tennis league winners c.1947. Left to right: Ernie Hine, Len Crozier, Fred Townley, Tony Winter, Alan Copelin.

Boxing, football, cricket, table tennis, rowing, gymnastics and other indoor activities were soon proving popular. Members were also encouraged to take part in a drama group which proved very successful. Revenue from the productions helped finance summer camps at South Coast and West Country resorts.

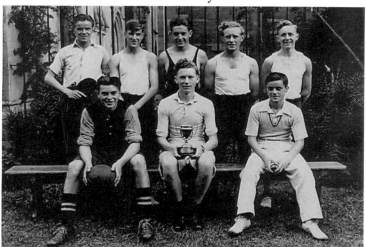

A member from each sporting activity that won the Oxford Mail Sports Trophy for best all round Boys' Club, c.1951. Back row: Ernie Hine (table tennis), Alan Barnes (gymnastics), Dennis Board (swimming), Eddie White (athletics), Ken Drew (cross country). Front row: Roy Gray (football), John Timms (rowing), Mick French (cricket).

Reading Boys Rowing Regatta c.1945. Winners of the Tub-Four. Back row: Fred Townley, Eddie White. Front row: John Timms, Alex Gibb (cox), Bruce Piper.

Gymnastic training c.1947.
Michael Botting
Ron Norris   Ray Watts   John Gray
John Bryden   Gilbert Hasledine

During the war years there were regular farewell parties as one by one members became eligible for national service. Evacuees staying in the area were taken into the club and, although unruly at first, soon became involved in all the club activities to good effect. Those older members who were unable to serve in the forces together with the evacuees kept the club going during the war years. Father Podmore went to serve as an army chaplain and was killed at Dunkirk.

Father Hemmings, who had been a leading light for many years, continued the good work and after the war St John's Boys' Club flourished in the sports and drama fields to the benefit of its members. There was a club for girls but they were only allowed to mix on special occasions.

Drama Production c.1949. Left to right: Roger Smith, Brian Bull, Ian Harper, Reg Bradshaw, Mike Botting, John Gray, Ken Barnes, Basil Morris.

The Club song, an introduction to the evening's entertainment, sung to the tune of 'Roll out the Barrel'.

1. *St John's Club speaking*
   Hello, hello everyone
   Here is our greeting
   We wish you a barrel of
   fun.

2. *We are a mixed lot*
   Coming from near and far
   So if you'll listen to our
   singing
   You will know who we are.

3. *We're the Juniors—Senior*
   Section
   And a jolly fine collection
   For we never need correction
   We're the best without
   exception.

4. *We play football, we play*
   cricket
   Father Dalby says we're
   wicked
   That's because we make
   more noise
   Than any other boys.

5. *So here we all are*
   We are the boys of St John's
   We bid you welcome
   Parents, friends, teachers and
   Dons.

6. *We hope to give you*
   An evening well worth your
   while
   So take your seats now get
   ready
   Just to laugh, scream and
   smile.

Minor football team c.1950–51 after 3–3 draw with Headington United Minors. Back row: Basil Morris, Peter Rathbone, Mick Skinner, George Mason, Alan Appleton, Pete Baiden. Front row: Fred Ealey, Alan Pavier, Brian Toms, Michael Botting, John Gray.

The Gladiator Club

Father David Hemmings.

The Cowley Fathers ran the successful St John's Boys' Club but the war years took away many of the older boys. When the war was over and a lot of the boys returned there was no adult club for them to attend. A committee was formed under the guidance of Father David Hemmings to look for suitable premises in which to form the club. In the Spring of 1946, 263 Iffley Road was vacated by the army and Father Hemmings persuaded the Society of St John The Evangelist to purchase the property for use as an adult club. This they agreed to do if part of the building was used as living accommodation. With this stipulation in place the project was started.

Drama Production, *You Can't Take It With You,* 1948. Left to right: Roy Masters, Jack Buck, Frank Pateman, Alex Gibb (seated), Chris Frances, Stuart Wilkins, Muriel Sewell, Roy Copeman, Eileen Wicks.

Table Tennis Team c.1953.
Ernie Hine   Ken Barson
Margaret Jeffrey Jack Leatherby
Tom Duckett.

Jack Leatherby
    Oxford District Table Tennis
    Assoc. Singles Champion
Ken Barson and Jack Leatherby
    Doubles Champions
Ernie Hine and Margaret Jeffrey
    Mixed Doubles Runners up

The Club was advertised and volunteers came forward to start the necessary work. Under the Chairman of the Committee, Mr Alec Gibb, a number of old members of St John's Boys' and Girls' Clubs started work.

After many weeks of dedicated work the Gladiator Club was opened on Saturday 4th October 1947. The name of the club came from a sign over a door when they took over the premises.

Over the years, when expansion was needed, the members pulled together to do much of the work themselves, often using reclaimed architectural material like the floor from the ballroom of the Clarendon Hotel. The club has seen many alterations over the years and still remains a successfully run club.

Tramps Ball c.1965. Dola Brooks, Shirley Blay, Margaret Garvey.

Wild West Fancy Dress Party c.1966.

Successful activites over the years included darts, badminton, hockey, mixed hockey, table tennis, squash, angling, basketball, football, cricket and also drama. The drama group was very successful and under Roy and Philip Copeman produced many plays and entered drama competitions. Patrick Mower and Bob Kingswell, who were members of the drama group, are now successful actors.

Summer camps became very well supported by the young families and became an annual event with up to sixty members in attendance.

Summer camp Guernsey c.1959.   Summer camp Jersey c.1957.

Shops and Businesses

Eli Smart, Undertaker

Eli Smart, always known as Jack, started an undertaking business in outhouses at the rear of Bartlemas Cottage, later moving to premises at the corner of George Street (now Hendred Street) and Oxford Road, Cowley. This wedding photograph taken in 1905 shows Eli and his wife either side of the bride and groom, Jessie North and Willie Smart. Left to right, back row: Dolly Smart with husband Bill Slingsby, Elizabeth Jane Smart, Harry Smart, Philip James Smart with wife Clara (née Smart), Tom Smart, George North, being one of the two younger lads, the other unknown. Middle row: Grace and Fred North, Eli, Jessie North, Willie Roland Smart, Francis Annie Smart (née Parrott), unknown lady. Front row: Gertie North, Ivy Smart, May Smart. The family lived at 20 Southfield Road.

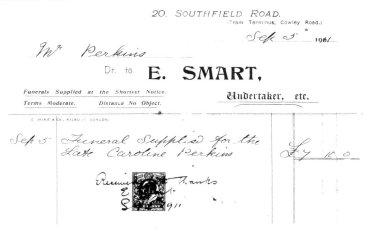

Jack Buckler, Fishmonger and Poulterer

Jack and his son Stan in the doorway of 168 Cowley Road, Christmas 1913. Many of the top rows of poultry and rabbits were left out overnight and guarded by a night-watchman who had a brazier to keep warm.

Jack Buckler learnt his trade from his father, Sam Buckler, who had a fishmonger's shop in the city centre.

In 1907 Jack started his own business at 168 Cowley Road and his son Stan, when he was old enough, joined the business. Jack ran the business until 1936 when Stan took over the reins.

Gordon Thompson started work at the shop in 1956 and when Stan retired in 1960 Gordon bought the business. He kept it going despite opposition from the super-markets, but when he retired in 1993 the business closed.

Jack, with son Stan and Stan's wife Mina, Christmas 1928.

Stan Buckler related the following story to Gordon Thompson.

One Christmas morning when Stan was young, he was looking forward to the Christmas dinner which was cooking in the kitchen. There was a knock at the front door; the caller was a customer of Jack Buckler's and he wanted to know why Jack had not delivered his turkey. It transpired that Jack had taken the order while on an evening out in the New Inn public house and had forgotten to write the order down.

As there was no poultry left, and not wanting to disappoint his customer, Jack gave him the family turkey cooking in their oven. Needless to say, Stan was devastated, his Christmas ending in tears.

THE FISHMONGER WHO HAD TO STAND IN A QUEUE!

A cartoon by Alan Course showing that Stan, although a fishmonger, had to queue like everyone else for his ration book after the war.

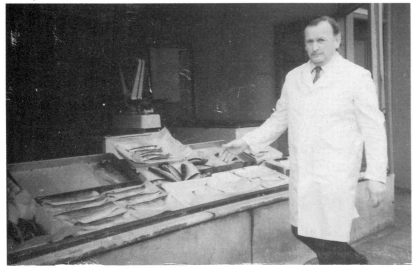

Gordon Thompson dressed for work.

Arthur Russen. The Landlord who delivered the mail.

The Temple Bar c.1910.

Arthur Russen came to Oxford in 1903 as landlord of the Temple Bar in Temple Street. This was one of his jobs, the other being a driver of the London to Oxford mail coach. Arthur used to set out for London at about 9.00 pm for the horse drawn coach journey of about 9 hours. The mail was collected from Mount Pleasant and lodgings obtained for the day. The return journey again started late evening, arriving at St Aldate's Post Office at about 6.00 a.m. Horses were changed en route and extra horses were provided on hilly sections.

At the Temple Bar there was a coach house with stables for the horses. Local children would often try to catch a ride on the step of the rear of the coach. Arthur was on duty in the Bar when not on the mail run.

The last journey of the parcel mail in 1905.

Arthur Russen at the wheel.

Arthur Russen was forced to give up the mail run following an accident with the horses and he then went into the car hire and taxi business.

Arthur's son, George, followed in his father's footsteps and drove one of the early Royal Mail motor vans during the First World War before taking over the running of the Temple Bar. Like his father, George also went into the taxi and haulage business with premises in St Mary's Road.

A publicity photograph for George Russen's St Mary's Road business.

East Oxford Schools

The rapidly expanding population in this Victorian suburb coincided with the government legislation of 1870 which aimed to make education available for all. School Boards were now enabled to supplement provision formerly undertaken by charities and religious bodies. Once schools were provided, then attendance was made compulsory and in 1880 all children were to attend full-time until the age of ten. Thus a problem of accommodation seems to have arisen and groups of children received their tuition in temporary premises until the major school sites were completed. The map below attempts to identify the position of the various educational establishments and the relevant dates in which they were in use.

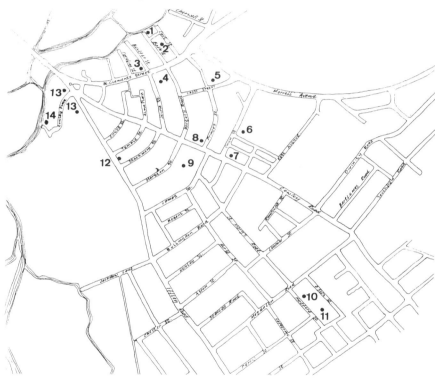

1.	Bath Street Infants School	1874–1956	8.	Cowley St John Mixed	1867–1872
2.	St Clement's Mixed School	1839–1911		Cowley St John Boys	1871–1872
3.	St Clement's Girls School	1891–1929	9.	Cowley St John Girls	1880–1932
4.	St Aloysius R.C. School	1795–	10.	St Mary and St John Boys	1896–1932
	St Aloysius Girls School	1825		St Mary and St John Girls	1896–1932
5.	St Clement's Boys School	1863–1900		St Mary and St John Juniors	1896–
6.	East Oxford Infant School	1902	11.	St Mary and St John Infants	1905–
	East Oxford Girls School	1902–1932	12.	St John's Middle Class School	c.1860
	East Oxford Boys School	1902–1932	13.	Magdalen College School	1893/4
7.	Cowley St John Infants	1873–1936	14.	Milham Ford School	1890s–1938

An aerial view of the north side of the Cowley Road showing the East Oxford School complex in 1940s. The two-storey building housed the Boys and Girls Schools (sexes were separated from the age of seven) and the single-storey building in the front was occupied by the infants. In the foreground on the main Cowley Road, to the right of the junction with Union Street, is the T-shaped Cowley St John Infant School.

Cowley St John Schools

The first Cowley St John School for boys and girls was started by Father Benson in 1867. It occupied a temporary wooden hut on the corner of Princes Street and a new permanent building was erected in 1871 on the same site which became the school for boys aged over 8 years. This remained as the Boys' School until it became the Community Centre. The Girls' School was situated between Marston Street and James Street. In 1872 a new Infant School was built to house 200 children aged between 5 and 8 years and occupied the site on the Cowley Road where Boots the Chemist is now.

Cowley St John Infant School c.1894 with Will Wilcox in his sailor suit in the front row second from the right.

Cowley St John Infant School, Class 3 in 1932. Left from the front: −, Doreen Higgs, − Colmer, −, −, 5 unknown, Fay Lander, −, − Redknap, Willy Sloper, −, −, −, Freddie Gomin, −, −. Right from the front: −, Grayson Hemmings, −, −, −, −, −, Vivienne Exchange, −, Raymond Brown, −, Melba Paddon, −, −, −, −, −, − Crapper, −, −, −, −, Wally King.

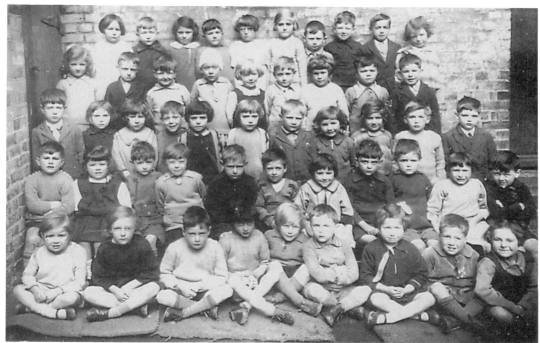

Cowley St John Infants in 1928. Back row: 6th from left Betty Spicer, 9th from left John Perry. Fourth row: 1st on left Violet Bannister, 4th Beryl Laurence, 5th Joan Bannister. Third row: 4th from left Graham Armstrong. Second row: 2nd from left Pamela Ashford(?). Front row: 1st on left Joan Hutt, 2nd Kath Pateman, 7th left Joan Lander, extreme right Peggy Lynes.

Cowley St John Boys School in 1928. The three boys in the grey shirts were from the Industrial Poor Law School, generally known as The Poplars. They were, from the left, P. Lambert, L. Drummond and R. Hewlett. — Rowland is 4th from the left at the back.

East Oxford School Site in Union Street

The School was designed by Leonard Stokes on behalf of the School Board in 1899. It was built on part of the brickwork site owned by Joseph Castle, whose Brick and Tile Works had been established there for over 40 years. There were three blocks; the single-storey building was designed for 160 infants and the two-storey building for 200 boys and 200 girls. It appears that in the 1930s the Girls School occupied the first floor and the Boys School the ground floor. The windows were placed high enough to prevent children from 'window gazing' and it is alleged that the stone sills on the ground floor were for the purpose of sharpening slate pencils used at the turn of the century. The building was occupied in 1900 and extended in 1902.

The site can be seen clearly in the aerial view on page 107 and the infant building can be seen on the right of the picture above with the former senior school on the left. By the date of this photograph in 1949 this was the junior school. The May celebration in progress has been an on-going tradition and the junior Morris Dancing Group can be seen waiting to perform.

The Infant May Celebration c.1912.

May Day in the 1920s. Back row: Margaret Osborn, Eileen Doubleday, Violet Hewers, Kathleen Smart, —. Front row: Hilda Hewers, Phyllis Owen.

East Oxford Infants c.1915 with Daisy Richardson third from the left in the fourth row.

East Oxford Girls School sewing class c. 1919 with Doris Richardson holding the name board.

A class of infants in 1926. Third row: Jack Masters, — Willis, —, —, Edelweiss Vistovski. Second row: 6th from left Rose —. Front row: 2nd from right Royston Beesley.

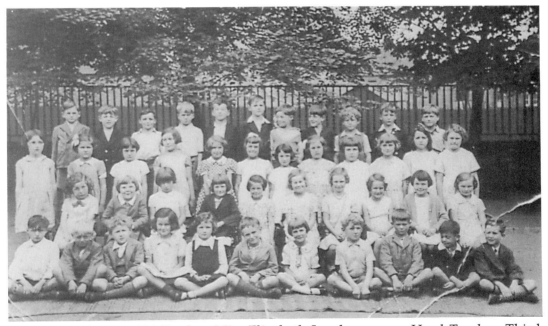

A class of infants c.1934/5 when Miss Elizabeth Lambourn was Head Teacher. Third row: June Westall, Mary Castle, Olive Morris, Beryl Hedges, — Scott, Pauline Earle, —, Marjorie Treen, Jean Howe, Betty Allaway, Hilda Butcher, Jean Hirons. Second row: Valerie Wheeler, Audrey Deacock, Phyllis Franklin, Jill —, Doreen Brocker, Elizabeth Beare, Iris Clegg, —, Pam Smith, Sheila Dunbar. Front row: —, —, —, Isabelle Pollard, Joan Crawte, —, —, Ross Skinner, Freddie Betteridge, —, —.

A class of infants in 1940. Back row: Hazel Russen, Brian Hounslow, –, –, Verna Whiting, Geoffrey Whoram, Rosemary Jones, –, Jean Timbs, –. Third row: Brian Seajull, Marion Stowe, John Howe, June Round, –, –, – King, – Quelch, Ken Drew, Barbara Clifford, –, June Bond. Second row: Alan Barnes, Myrtle King, –, Sheila King, –, June Mead, Kenneth Bull, Eileen Bournton, –, Jean Hodges. Front row: –, Gwen Rose, –, Peggy Brill, –, Cynthia Duckett, –, –, –.

Miss Jenner's class at the Junior School in Spring 1953. Back row: Martin Maycock, Shirley Norton, David Valender, J. Jones, Michael Crane, Glenys Howard, John Gapper, Patricia Pearman, Roy Pyniger, Diana Kent. Third row: Pamela Barnard, Michael Hickman, Pauline Hayward, Michael Millward, Elizabeth Wray, John Walters, Rosemary Tennant, Michael Webb, Julie Bryden, David Ludlow. Second row: Tony Jones, Susan Wiggins, Ian Johnson, Janet Mackay, James Cashmore, Gillian Harvey, Norman White, Susan Couling, Alan Davies, Daphne Broome. Front row: Caroline Shaw, Peter O'Dell, Susan Adey-Smith, David Harse, Carol Prior, R. Smart, Rita Padmore, Anthony Andrews, Christine Huish, Michael Jones.

Mr Scott's class during a football lesson on Angel Meadow 1944—5. Back row: Edwards, Drinkwater, Josephs, Hatton, Cox, Lee, Read, Cooper, Green, Jeffries. Middle: Harriman, Hall, Blackman, Gray, Russell, Bayliss, Jones, Woodward, Mason, Hall, Yendell, Parsons, Whittaker, Clarke, Harrison Front: Oswell, Williams, Butler, Tredwell, Smith, Freeman, Jones, Jennings, Maasz, Barnes, Clifford, Hookham.

East Oxford Junior School Football team 1952—3 in the year that they reached the semi-final of the City Schools Cup. The picture was taken in Cheney Lane Woods and the team regularly practised on the Marsh ground. Back row: David Ledger, Martin Maycock, Ian Moffit, Tony Hancock, Michael Walton, Alan Smith. Front row: Anthony Cross, Michael Webb, Dennis Urcott, Peter Coppock, Michael Jones.

School Celebrations at East Oxford

Fancy Dress Parade 1952 with Michael Pateman as a policeman.

Fancy Dress Parade to celebrate the Festival of Britain in 1951. From left to right, Glenys Howard, Shirley Norton, Julie Bryden, −, −, Roy Pyniger.

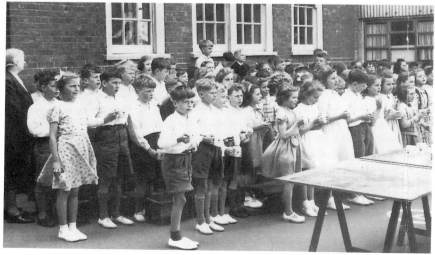

Coronation Mug Presentation in 1953 with Miss Tombs, Head Teacher, on the left.

Edward Arnold Greening Lamborn, Hon. M.A. Oxon. Schoolmaster and Antiquary, Headmaster of East Oxford Boys School 1908–1944

'There was born a man who was to make his mark on the minds and buttocks of countless numbers of boy pupils!' (Ramon Roper ex-pupil recalls.)

E.A.G. Lamborn was born the son of Arnold Lamborn and Susannah Greening in 1877 and spent his early life at 101 Cowley Road where his father carried out an insurance agency. 'Ikey', as Lamborn was known by his pupils, referred to himself as a self-educated man who gained his knowledge from *'good books, great buildings, all wild creatures and nature'.* His early education is unknown but it appears that he became a pupil teacher at the age of 15 and attended Culham College, Abingdon from 1897 to 1899, following in his father's footsteps who had been a student there in 1862–3.

Pencil sketch by E. Platchey 1939. which used to hang in the school hall.

'Ikey' has been described as *'a slight figure with an aura of confidence, capable of extreme sarcasm (his favourite weapon) but of complete sympathy in situations requiring it'.* He walked with a distinct bouncing gait which was highlighted by his bright red or yellow socks, and he was a quietly strict disciplinarian.

101, Cowley Road pictured in 1993. (It was formerly No. 43 before being renumbered in 1893). This was the home of the Lamborn family in the 1880s when E.A. Greening Lamborn was a boy. His father was a valuer in the insurance business and worked from these premises. They were later to become Silk's Grocers and Confectioners and have latterly returned to their original use as John Roberts & Co. Insurance Consultants.

On the left is the earliest known photograph of E.A. Greening Lamborn. His first teaching post seems to have been at St Mary Magdalen School near Gloucester Green where he taught from 1900 to 1908. He was then appointed to the post of Headmaster at the East Oxford Boys School where he was to remain for 36 years.

20 Cowley Road, a small terraced house which Lamborn bought c. 1900 while he was teaching at St Mary Magdalen School.

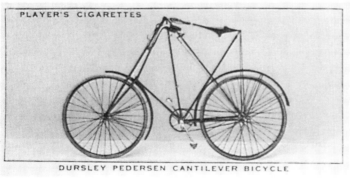

PLAYER'S CIGARETTES

DURSLEY PEDERSEN CANTILEVER BICYCLE

Lamborn used to cycle to East Oxford School on one of these bicycles and one of the most prestigious positions was to be appointed as Ikey's personal bicycle monitor; the duties involved cleaning, oiling and inflating the tyres (reproduced by curtesy of the Imperial Tobacco Co.).

E.A. Greening Lamborn was an educational revolutionary; he scrapped the then widely accepted 'civil service' handwriting script and encouraged boys to think creatively, placing great emphasis on poetry, the study of nature and architecture. He was merciless over slipshod grammar. He firmly believed in learning from first-hand experience and Tuckwell's lorries were hired to transport boys into the countryside for lectures and practical activities. One such trip is remembered by an ex-pupil.

'This was a Thames tow-path walk from Oxford to Radley. A pause for swimming in the river was taken about one mile down-stream from Sandford. Lamborn dressed himself in a rather ancient style swimming costume, then swam in a very strong side-stroke. Returning to the river bank to dress, he found that a hungry cow had devoured much of his trousers. A pair of nail scissors reduced the ragged legs to leave a strange pair of shorts'.

He shared his enthusiasms for local history, topography, architecture, heraldry and wildlife with his pupils, inspiring many of them with interests which would last for the rest of their lives. Lamborn was himself a prolific writer and has left many acclaimed volumes, some of which are listed below.

The Story of Architecture in Oxford Stone, 1912.

Shakespeare, the Man and his Stage, in collaberation with Dr G.B. Harrison, 1924.

A School History of Berkshire, 1908.

Armorial Glass in the Oxford Diocese 1250–1850, 1949.

The Ancestry of Mr Winston Churchill, 1944.

Heraldry and the History of Parliament, 1945.

The Parish Church, 1929.

Reason in Arithmetic, 1930.

Lamborn in his caravan, August 1950, in which he relaxed and studied the countryside. The caravan was situated in an isolated spot and he is seen above with a smile on his face, an expression seldom seen by his pupils.

Lamborn was considered to be the greatest antiquary since Anthony Wood. He was also a part-time inspector for the Board of Education.

E.A. Greening Lamborn was a teacher with vision, *'an educator of the education officials'*; the Inspectors would call when he was out as they were wary of his progressive methods. However, they acknowledged his successes as illustrated below.

'Among the impressive characteristics of this school are the high standard of effort demanded by thought-compelling teaching; the general keenness, vigour and freedom of the boys, not exclusive of the slower witted ones: the zealous work of the staff on lines inspired and exemplified by the Headmaster with marked intellectual power: the self reliance, workmanlike application and good progress of the private study group, in which every promising boy is placed as young as possible under supervision which at once encourages the boy and keeps before them an ideal of scholarly work.'

Board of Education Report, 23rd May 1927.

Lamborn's brightest pupils in the private study group which was held in the main hall. Back row: Lamborn, Norman Dubber, –, –, – Blay. Fourth row: James –, –, –, –, Marsden Gray, Sam Burnett. Third row: –, Miss Forshaw, –, – Knight. Second row: –, –, Lewendon, –, Royston Beesley, Tony Smith. Front row: –, Walter Ing's (Deputy Head) son.

Lambourn's pupils remember him fondly. He was known to have paid for the uniforms of scholarship boys from his own pocket.

> *'Ikey Lamborn is a good man,*
> *Tries to teach you all he can,*
> *Read and write and arithmetic,*
> *And doesn't forget to give you the stick.'*

EAST OXFORD SCHOOL

Dinner

commemorate the Headmastership of the late
E. A. GREENING LAMBORN, ESQ., Hon. M.A.

TEMPLE FARM CLUB
SANDFORD-ON-THAMES
SATURDAY, NOV. 18TH, 1961

The Rt. Worshipful the Mayor of Oxford
(Ald. Lionel Harrison) presiding

Toasts	*Menu*
THE QUEEN	Cream of Tomato Soup
—	—
"IKEY"	Roast Sirloin of Beef
Proposed by the Rt. Worshipful the Mayor	Yorkshire Pudding
	Roast Potatoes
	Brussels Sprouts
—	—
THE SCHOOL	Pears and Fresh Cream
Proposed by John Owen	—
Response by W. F. Martin, Esq. (Headmaster)	Cheese and Biscuits
	—
	Coffee

The commemorative dinner programme held in 1961 with 39 ex-pupils' signatures.

St Mary and St John Schools

This school site was purchased in the 1890s and was funded by Father Benson and the Cowley Fathers in order to *'keep Godless Board Schools out of the area'*. According to the logbook the Boys School opened on the 16th January 1893 with 22 boys in a temporary building and the main brick building was completed in 1896, being enlarged in 1898 to house 340 boys. The Boys' School occupied the ground floor with an entrance from Hertford Street and the Girls' School for 340 girls occupied the first floor with an entrance in Essex Street. The Infant School next door was completed in 1905 with provision for 400 children. These youngsters had previously been accommodated in St Mary's Road and the school had been given the nickname of the Robin Hood School, which reflects the notoriety of the area at this time. In 1932 the school became an infant and junior school and the senior pupils transferred to the Cowley St John Schools.

The girls' playground and entrance in 1910.

A view of the splendid infant school hall designed by John Ninian Comper with a P. E. lesson in progress c.1940s.

A group of tambourine players in 1903.

The May Queen and her attendants c.1900 with Lucy Jeffery of Sidney Street standing second from the left.

A class of boys in 1904.

ARTHUR LEONARD JEFFERY

8. 10. 08.

My Autobiography.

I was born at Oxford in the year 1896 and am therefore twelve years old. My father is a gasfitter. I started school at the age of three at S.t Mary and John Infant School. I was transferred to the big boys' school at the age of seven. I am now in standard six. The lessons I like best are chemistry and drawing especially the former. I shall be leaving school in about a year and a half; halfs time and I hope to be a college servant. In the morning before school I generally run mothers errands. (At 1) In the

evening after tea I go on to the Recreation Ground (and) to have a game at cricket or football and I go to bed about nine oclock. On Saturdays I generally clean the knives, run mothers errands and help mother in her household work in the morning and I generally have the rest of the day to myself. When I leave school I don't (ero) expect to encounter such happy days as I have during my schooldays

Good

The autobiography of Arthur Jeffery written in 1908 while he was pupil at the school.

A group of girls in 1915 with Mabel Walton in the centre.

Lucy Jeffery, third from left, in 1910 in the girls' playground.

St Mary and St John infants in 1926. Back row: Nancy Clinkard, Hilda Bevill, 4 unknown. Fourth row: −, Elsie Brown, Ann Morgan, Renee Simms, 3 unknown. Third row: −, Gwen Nash, −, Marjorie Busby, 3 unknown. Second row: −, Florrie Clark, Sylvia Tomlin, 4 unknown. Front row: −, −, −, Edith Newbold, −, Beryl Greason, −, Ken Greason (twins).

A group of infants in 1933 with Sheila Perkins on the swing. This classroom is where the swimming pool is now. None of the pupils remembers playing on the rocking horse or the swing!

The Girls School Staff c.1930. Back row: Miss Delamore, Miss Westall(?), Miss Walker(?), Miss Goodwin. Front row: Miss Mott, Mrs Gillett, Miss Seward (Headmistress), Miss Courtenay, M. Skinner.

The St Mary and St John percussion band performing at the Jubilee Celebrations in December 1935.

'A Jubilee entertainment organised by Miss M.N. Seward, Headmistress of the Girls School, took place on Tuesday evening and was attended by 250 parents and friends. Most of the 300 children in the school played some part and a children's band was conducted by Jean Robinson aged eight.The programme included songs, recitations, violin selections, school games and an exhibition of country dancing; none of the performers was over eleven. The proceeds were in aid of the School Appeal Fund.'

Local Newspaper Report.

The school allotments 1934—35. The plot of land used to teach the boys gardening skills was situated in an area called Boundary Brook Close. It was opposite Donnington Bridge Road and backed onto Howard Street.

A group of eight year olds in 1935 believed to be at the school. Unfortunately, the focus of the event is lost to living memory. They have been wrongly identified in the past as wartime evacuees. Back row: Jean Sumner, Pam Buller, Josie — , Gladys Parsons, Eileen Bullock, Stanley —, —, Sheila Coles, —, —. Front row: Sheila Perkins, —, Betty Allen, —, —, Jean Cornborough, —, —.

St Mary and St John Junior School 1934, aged 10 years. Back row: Sybil King, Nora Stimpson, Mary Rawlings, —, Barbara Mansell, Gladys Kinch, Dorothy Gardner. Third row: —, —, Marion Jefferies, Joan Rawlings, Beryl Fowler, Mary Millin, Barbara Kingston, Peggy Townsend. Second row: Catherine Farnell, Mavis Flood, (the next five girls include Beryl Filer, Joan Meadows, Eileen Hector, Sheila Dashwood), Dorothy Brown, —, Olga Veary, —. Front row: Doreen Holland, —, —, Ruth Gurden, —, Monica Townsend, Minny Bolton.